THIS BOOK BELONGS TO

_____

_____

START DATE _____/_____/_____

HE READS TRUTH

FOUNDERS

FOUNDER
Raechel Myers

CO-FOUNDER
Amanda Bible Williams

EXECUTIVE

CHIEF EXECUTIVE OFFICER
Ryan Myers

CHIEF OPERATING OFFICER
Mark D. Bullard

EDITORIAL

MANAGING EDITOR
Lindsey Jacobi, MDiv

PRODUCTION EDITOR
Hannah Little, MTS

ASSOCIATE EDITOR
Kayla De La Torre, MAT

COPY EDITOR
Becca Owens, MA

CREATIVE

SENIOR ART DIRECTOR
Annie Glover

DESIGN MANAGER
Kelsea Allen

DESIGNERS
Savannah Ault
Ashley Phillips

MARKETING

MARKETING LEAD
Kelsey Chapman

PRODUCT MARKETING MANAGER
Krista Squibb

CONTENT MARKETING STRATEGIST
Tameshia Williams, ThM

SOCIAL MEDIA SPECIALIST
Bella Ponce

OPERATIONS

OPERATIONS DIRECTOR
Allison Sutton

OPERATIONS MANAGER
Mary Beth Steed

GROUP SALES AND
ENGAGEMENT SPECIALIST
Karson Speth

COMMUNITY ENGAGEMENT

COMMUNITY ENGAGEMENT
MANAGER
Delaney Coleman

COMMUNITY ENGAGEMENT
SPECIALISTS
Cait Baggerman
Katy McKnight

SHIPPING

SHIPPING MANAGER
Marian Welch

FULFILLMENT LEAD
Hannah Song

FULFILLMENT SPECIALIST
Kelsey Simpson

CONTRIBUTORS

SPECIAL THANKS
John Greco, MDiv
Jessica Lamb, MA
Melanie Rainer, MATS
Kara Gause
Ellen Taylor

SUBSCRIPTION INQUIRIES
orders@hereadstruth.com

COLOPHON

This book was printed in Nashville, Tennessee, on 60# Lynx Opaque Text under the direction of He Reads Truth. Cover is 100# Cougar Opaque with a soft touch lamination.

HEREADSTRUTH.COM

@HEREADSTRUTH

Download the He Reads Truth app, available for iOS and Android

PEOPLE IN THE OLD TESTAMENT

HE READS TRUTH

GOD IS AT WORK
IN EVERY STORY.

Y ou know those moments as a Bible reader when something jumps off the page for the first time? It may be a passage or a story you've read ten times before, but this time, you see it—something you have never noticed before. It can be a jarring feeling, reading something so familiar and yet still finding something new.

That's one of many beautiful aspects of being in relationship with our God—we can know Him intimately and at the same time always have something new to learn about Him. We can spend our whole lives following Him, and still find fresh exhilaration in the timeless stories of His goodness and faithful love.

That is the driving force behind the reading plan in your hands. We want to look at the lives of men and women in the Old Testament—some who may be familiar, and some who may be new names to you—and see the evidence of the Lord's deep and specific faithfulness in every story. He was there, present with His people to bring hope and life in seemingly impossible situations. Not vaguely and theoretically, but specifically and actually.

We know this because the whole of Scripture tells us so: The Lord is near to the brokenhearted (Ps 34:18). He loves justice (Ps 37:28), and He hates sin (Ps 11:5; Pr 6:12-19). He is compassionate and gracious, all-knowing and all-powerful (Ex 34:6; Jr 32:17; 1Jn 3:20), and He dispels darkness with the light of life (Jn 1:5; 10:10). This is the God who is present in the stories you'll read over the next seven weeks, and in our own. Our study will focus on women and men in the Old Testament, with key questions at the end of each day designed to direct our gaze to God, the hero of every story.

Our team has assembled an intentionally-crafted, thoughtful book to guide you through this seven-week reading plan. The introductory essays, beginning on page 15, provide a biblically sound framework for engaging this diverse group of stories. Don't miss "Connecting the Stories" on page 116, an extra created to help us understand how the people we will read about are connected to one another in the larger story of the Old Testament.

God is at work in every story. May your time spent reading about men and women in the Old Testament draw you into deeper relationship with Him, teaching you to trust and recognize His good hand in these stories and in your own.

THE HE READS TRUTH TEAM

DESIGN ON PURPOSE

Each He Reads Truth resource is thoughtfully and artfully designed to highlight the beauty, goodness, and truth of Scripture in a way that reflects the themes of each curated reading plan.

The art throughout this book was created by our team using a variety of mediums and tools—like colored pencils, oil pastels, and wax crayons—to represent how God uses all kinds of people and their unique stories, talents, and shortcomings to play a role in His story. The bright colors of the abstract art are paired with black and white lifestyle photography to further highlight the wonder of God using everyday, ordinary people to build His kingdom.

HOW TO USE THIS BOOK

He Reads Truth is a community of men dedicated to reading the Word of God every day. In the **People in the Old Testament** reading plan, we will study the stories of men and women in the Old Testament to see God at work in the lives of His people and the world.

READ & REFLECT

Your **People in the Old Testament** book focuses primarily on Scripture, with added features to come alongside your time with God's Word.

SCRIPTURE READING

Designed for a Monday start, this book presents daily readings from the stories of Old Testament men and women.

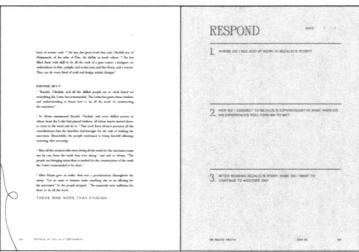

REFLECTION QUESTIONS

Each weekday features questions and space for personal reflection.

COMMUNITY & CONVERSATION

You can start reading this book at any time. If you want to join men from across the globe as they read along with you, the He Reads Truth community will start Day 1 of **People in the Old Testament** on Monday, May 5, 2025.

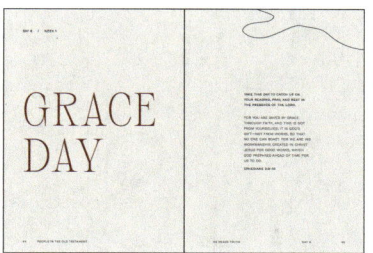

GRACE DAY

Use Saturdays to catch up on your reading, pray, and rest in the presence of the Lord.

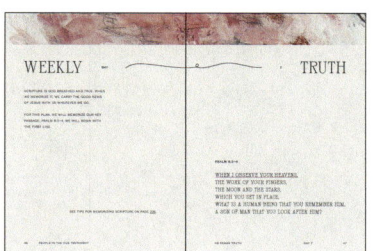

WEEKLY TRUTH

Sundays are set aside for Scripture memorization.

See tips for memorizing Scripture on page 236.

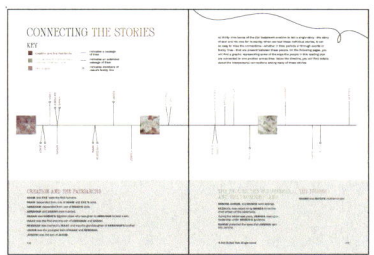

EXTRAS

This book features additional tools to help you gain a deeper understanding of the text.

Find a complete list of extras on page 13.

HE READS TRUTH APP

Devotionals corresponding to each daily reading can be found in the **People in the Old Testament** reading plan on the He Reads Truth app. Devotionals will be published each weekday once the plan begins on Monday, May 5, 2025. You can use the app to participate in community discussion and more.

HEREADSTRUTH.COM

The **People in the Old Testament** reading plan and devotionals will also be available at HeReadsTruth.com as the community reads each day. Invite your family, friends, and neighbors to read along with you.

TABLE OF CONTENTS

INTRODUCTION

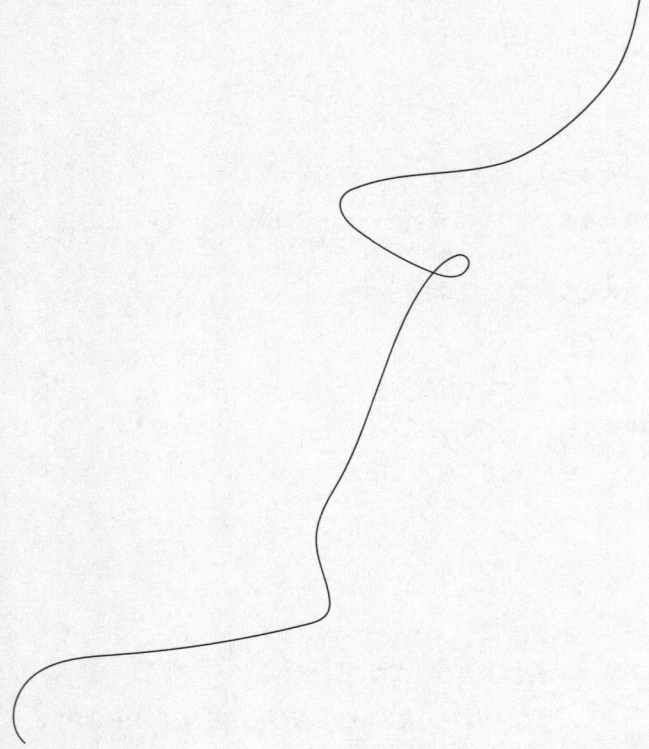

WHEN I OBSERVE YOUR HEAVENS, THE WORK OF YOUR FINGERS, THE
MOON AND THE STARS, WHICH YOU SET IN PLACE, WHAT IS A HUMAN
BEING THAT YOU REMEMBER HIM, A SON OF MAN THAT YOU LOOK
AFTER HIM?

PSALM 8:3–4

WHY READ THE STORIES OF PEOPLE IN THE BIBLE?

All of the people included in the Bible are there for a reason. They are meant to be remembered, and we are meant to read their stories. Scripture reminds us that what was written is for our instruction so we might have hope and encouragement (Rm 15:4). The Bible is a gift for us to open, engage with, and learn from.

WHICH PEOPLE IN THE BIBLE?

The women and men in this study are not the "greatest hits" of the Old Testament, but they're not a collection of completely unknown stories either. In this reading plan, you'll find a variety of intentionally selected people whose narratives remind us that we can learn about God through every story in Scripture.

The people we'll read about are presented largely in chronological order, though some narratives may be slightly out of order to focus on a particular person's part in a larger story. Each reading day stands on its own, and these stories can be revisited in any order. As you read, you'll notice that the reading days differ vastly in length. Some days contain the full biblical, historical record of a person while others represent a curated selection of readings for those whose narrative accounts contain more than could be easily read within a day. Keep in mind that each day serves to best represent a person's life, but it may not encapsulate every facet from the biblical record.

OUR HOPE FOR THIS READING PLAN

As we focus our Bible reading for the next seven weeks on several people in the Old Testament—a set of imperfect people included by God in His grand story of redemption—our ultimate goal is to see God at work each day in the pages of Scripture. We want to know God more deeply and worship Him wholeheartedly by reading each of these accounts.

As men in the Word, we want to grow and be changed by what we read. After each day's reading, you'll find space to reflect on and respond to all God is teaching you through His Word. We hope this study encourages you to take a deeper look into the lives of the people we've selected and inspires you to read about the people we have not explored in this study. Remember to take what you'll read into your daily life, allowing God's Word to encourage, influence, and strengthen you and the people you interact with.

HOW TO READ STORIES OF PEOPLE IN THE BIBLE

THE BIBLE IS GOD'S STORY, BUT IT'S ALSO THE STORY OF WOMEN AND MEN WHO PLAYED UNIQUE ROLES IN REDEMPTION HISTORY. HERE ARE SOME PRINCIPLES TO KEEP IN MIND AS YOU READ ABOUT THE LIVES OF PEOPLE IN THE BIBLE.

BIBLICAL NARRATIVE IS OFTEN DESCRIPTIVE RATHER THAN PRESCRIPTIVE.

The stories are often not intended to be viewed as positive or examples to follow but a record of events in the history of God's people.

THE WOMEN AND MEN IN THE BIBLE ARE COMPLEX.

People rarely fall into neat categories of good or bad. Jesus alone is wholly good.

OUR SOCIAL NORMS ARE DIFFERENT FROM THOSE WE ENCOUNTER IN THE BIBLE.

God spoke into culture as it existed, and it is important to keep in mind that not all practices found in Scripture (e.g., polygamy, slavery) were part of God's design for His creation. At the same time, we remember that, though human laws and customs vary over time, His eternal wisdom remains unchanged.

GOD'S REVELATION IS GRADUAL.

Since we have the complete Old and New Testaments, we benefit from knowledge about certain aspects of God's plan that the women and men we read about in Scripture did not.

GOD WORKED THROUGH BROKEN, SINFUL PEOPLE.

And He still does! While it may be easy to judge or condemn the people in Scripture, remember that these were actual people with complex experiences. We draw hope from the ways God used these real lives to bring about His redemption story.

ADAM & EVE

GOD'S FIRST IMAGE-BEARERS

So God created man
in his own image;
he created him in the image of God;
he created them male and female.

GENESIS 2:4–9, 15–25

MAN AND WOMAN IN THE GARDEN

[4] These are the records of the heavens and the earth, concerning their creation. At the time that the LORD God made the earth and the heavens, [5] no shrub of the field had yet grown on the land, and no plant of the field had yet sprouted, for the LORD God had not made it rain on the land, and there was no man to work the ground. [6] But mist would come up from the earth and water all the ground. [7] Then the LORD God formed the man out of the dust from the ground and breathed the breath of life into his nostrils, and the man became a living being.

[8] The LORD God planted a garden in Eden, in the east, and there he placed the man he had formed. [9] The LORD God caused to grow out of the ground every tree pleasing in appearance and good for food, including the tree of life in the middle of the garden, as well as the tree of the knowledge of good and evil.

…

[15] THE LORD GOD TOOK THE MAN AND PLACED HIM IN THE GARDEN OF EDEN TO WORK IT AND WATCH OVER IT.

[16] And the LORD God commanded the man, "You are free to eat from any tree of the garden, [17] but you must not eat from the tree of the knowledge of good and evil, for on the day you eat from it, you will certainly die." [18] Then the LORD God said, "It is not good for the man to be alone. I will make a helper corresponding to him." [19] The LORD God formed out of the ground every wild animal and every bird of the sky, and brought each to the man to see what he would call it. And whatever the man called a living creature, that was its name. [20] The man gave names to all the livestock, to the birds of the sky, and to every wild animal; but for the man no helper was found corresponding to him. [21] So the LORD God caused a deep sleep to come over the man, and he slept. God took one of his ribs and closed the flesh at that place. [22] Then the LORD God made

the rib he had taken from the man into a woman and brought her to the man. [23] And the man said:

> This one, at last, is bone of my bone
> and flesh of my flesh;
> this one will be called "woman,"
> for she was taken from man.

[24] This is why a man leaves his father and mother and bonds with his wife, and they become one flesh. [25] Both the man and his wife were naked, yet felt no shame.

GENESIS 3

THE TEMPTATION AND THE FALL

[1] Now the serpent was the most cunning of all the wild animals that the LORD God had made. He said to the woman, "Did God really say, 'You can't eat from any tree in the garden'?"

[2] The woman said to the serpent, "We may eat the fruit from the trees in the garden. [3] But about the fruit of the tree in the middle of the garden, God said, 'You must not eat it or touch it, or you will die.'"

[4] "No! You will certainly not die," the serpent said to the woman. [5] "In fact, God knows that when you eat it your eyes will be opened and you will be like God, knowing good and evil." [6] The woman saw that the tree was good for food and delightful to look at, and that it was desirable for obtaining wisdom. So she took some of its fruit and ate it; she also gave some to her husband, who was with her, and he ate it. [7] Then the eyes of both of them were opened, and they knew they were naked; so they sewed fig leaves together and made coverings for themselves.

SIN'S CONSEQUENCES

[8] Then the man and his wife heard the sound of the LORD God walking in the garden at the time of the evening breeze, and they hid from the LORD God among the trees of the garden. [9] So the LORD God called out to the man and said to him, "Where are you?"

[10] And he said, "I heard you in the garden, and I was afraid because I was naked, so I hid."

[11] Then he asked, "Who told you that you were naked? Did you eat from the tree that I commanded you not to eat from?"

[12] The man replied, "The woman you gave to be with me—she gave me some fruit from the tree, and I ate."

[13] So the LORD God asked the woman, "What have you done?"

And the woman said, "The serpent deceived me, and I ate."

[14] So the LORD God said to the serpent:

> Because you have done this,
> you are cursed more than any livestock
> and more than any wild animal.
> You will move on your belly
> and eat dust all the days of your life.
> [15] I will put hostility between you and the woman,
> and between your offspring and her offspring.
> He will strike your head,
> and you will strike his heel.

[16] He said to the woman:

> I will intensify your labor pains;
> you will bear children with painful effort.
> Your desire will be for your husband,
> yet he will rule over you.

[17] And he said to the man, "Because you listened to your wife and ate from the tree about which I commanded you, 'Do not eat from it':

> The ground is cursed because of you.
> You will eat from it by means of painful labor
> all the days of your life.
> [18] It will produce thorns and thistles for you,
> and you will eat the plants of the field.
> [19] You will eat bread by the sweat of your brow
> until you return to the ground,
> since you were taken from it.
> For you are dust,
> and you will return to dust."

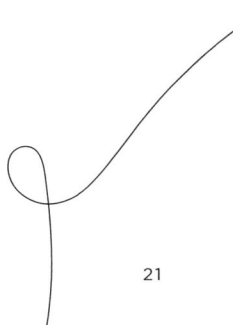

[20] The man named his wife Eve because she was the mother of all the living. [21] The LORD God made clothing from skins for the man and his wife, and he clothed them.

[22] The LORD God said, "Since the man has become like one of us, knowing good and evil, he must not reach out, take from the tree of life, eat, and live forever." [23] So the LORD God sent him away from the garden of Eden to work the ground from which he was taken. [24] He drove the man out and stationed the cherubim and the flaming, whirling sword east of the garden of Eden to guard the way to the tree of life.

GENESIS 5:1-2

[1] This is the document containing the family records of Adam. On the day that God created man, he made him in the likeness of God; [2] he created them male and female. When they were created, he blessed them and called them mankind.

RESPOND

DATE   /   /

After each day's reading, use these questions to engage with the text and reflect on what you've read. As you come to these questions every day, you may not always have an answer for each one. Use whichever ones help you best respond to God's Word.

1. WHERE DO I SEE GOD AT WORK IN ADAM AND EVE'S STORY?

Throughout this reading plan, you'll notice that God accomplishes His great story through imperfect people in different ways. As you consider this question each day, look for the themes that arise that set this person apart from those around them. How might God have been working in their life uniquely?

2. HOW DO I CONNECT TO ADAM AND EVE'S EXPERIENCES? IN WHAT WAYS DO THEIR EXPERIENCES FEEL FOREIGN TO ME?

Though we are separated by time and culture, these men and women are not that different from us—they held jobs, shared meals, and navigated challenging situations in life. Consider how you may not be as different from them as you might have previously thought, and contrast that with any parts of their story that are unique to their context.

3. AFTER READING ADAM AND EVE'S STORY, WHAT DO I WANT TO CONTINUE TO MEDITATE ON?

As you engage with the narratives in this reading plan, you may encounter details, tensions, or dialogue that spark a question, some confusion, or even some intrigue. Whether it is a truth to take to heart or a question to dive deeper into, use this space to record how you want to reflect on the day's Scripture passages moving forward. (You can even use this time to dig into other parts of this person's story throughout Scripture.)

NOAH

GENESIS 5:28–29

²⁸ Lamech was 182 years old when he fathered a son. ²⁹ And he named him Noah, saying, "This one will bring us relief from the agonizing labor of our hands, caused by the ground the LORD has cursed."

GENESIS 6:9–22

GOD WARNS NOAH

⁹ These are the family records of Noah. Noah was a righteous man, blameless among his contemporaries; Noah walked with God. ¹⁰ And Noah fathered three sons: Shem, Ham, and Japheth.

¹¹ Now the earth was corrupt in God's sight, and the earth was filled with wickedness. ¹² God saw how corrupt the earth was, for every creature had corrupted its way on the earth. ¹³ Then God said to Noah, "I have decided to put an end to every creature, for the earth is filled with wickedness because of them; therefore I am going to destroy them along with the earth.

¹⁴ "Make yourself an ark of gopher wood. Make rooms in the ark, and cover it with pitch inside and outside. ¹⁵ This is how you are to make it: The ark will be 450 feet long, 75 feet wide, and 45 feet high. ¹⁶ You are to make a roof, finishing the sides of the ark to within eighteen inches of the roof. You are to put a door in the side of the ark. Make it with lower, middle, and upper decks.

¹⁷ "Understand that I am bringing a flood—floodwaters on the earth to destroy every creature under heaven with the breath of life in it. Everything on earth will perish. ¹⁸ But I will establish my covenant with you, and you will enter the ark with your sons, your wife, and your sons' wives. ¹⁹ You are also to bring into the ark two of all the living creatures, male and female, to keep them alive with you. ²⁰ Two of everything—from the birds according to their kinds, from the livestock according to their kinds, and from the animals that crawl on the ground according to their kinds—will come to you so that you can keep them alive. ²¹ Take with you every kind of food that is eaten; gather it as food for you and for them." ²² And Noah did this. He did everything that God had commanded him.

GENESIS 7:6–12

⁶ Noah was six hundred years old when the flood came and water covered the earth. ⁷ So Noah, his sons, his wife, and his sons' wives

entered the ark because of the floodwaters. [8] From the animals that are clean, and from the animals that are not clean, and from the birds and every creature that crawls on the ground, [9] two of each, male and female, came to Noah and entered the ark, just as God had commanded him. [10] Seven days later the floodwaters came on the earth.

THE FLOOD

[11] In the six hundredth year of Noah's life, in the second month, on the seventeenth day of the month, on that day all the sources of the vast watery depths burst open, the floodgates of the sky were opened, [12] and the rain fell on the earth forty days and forty nights.

GENESIS 8:13-22

[13] In the six hundred first year, in the first month, on the first day of the month, the water that had covered the earth was dried up. Then Noah removed the ark's cover and saw that the surface of the ground was drying. [14] By the twenty-seventh day of the second month, the earth was dry.

THE LORD'S PROMISE

[15] Then God spoke to Noah, [16] "Come out of the ark, you, your wife, your sons, and your sons' wives with you. [17] Bring out all the living creatures that are with you—birds, livestock, those that crawl on the earth—and they will spread over the earth and be fruitful and multiply on the earth." [18] So Noah, along with his sons, his wife, and his sons' wives, came out. [19] All the animals, all the creatures that crawl, and all the flying creatures—everything that moves on the earth—came out of the ark by their families.

[20] Then Noah built an altar to the LORD. He took some of every kind of clean animal and every kind of clean bird and offered burnt offerings on the altar. [21] When the LORD smelled the pleasing aroma, he said to himself, "I will never again curse the ground because of human beings, even though the inclination of the human heart is evil from youth onward. And I will never again strike down every living thing as I have done.

[22] As long as the earth endures,
seedtime and harvest, cold and heat,
summer and winter, and day and night
will not cease."

GENESIS 9:1-17

GOD'S COVENANT WITH NOAH

[1] God blessed Noah and his sons and said to them, "Be fruitful and multiply and fill the earth. [2] The fear and terror of you will be in every living creature on the earth, every bird of the sky, every creature that crawls on the ground, and all the fish of the sea. They are placed under your authority. [3] Every creature that lives and moves will be food for you; as I gave the green plants, I have given you everything. [4] However, you must not eat meat with its lifeblood in it. [5] And I will require a penalty for your lifeblood; I will require it from any animal and from any human; if someone murders a fellow human, I will require that person's life.

[6] Whoever sheds human blood,
by humans his blood will be shed,
for God made humans in his image.

[7] But you, be fruitful and multiply; spread out over the earth and multiply on it."

[8] Then God said to Noah and his sons with him, [9] "Understand that I am establishing my covenant with you and your descendants after you, [10] and with every living creature that is with you—birds, livestock, and all wildlife of the earth that are with you—all the animals of the earth that came out of the ark. [11] I establish my covenant with you that never again will every creature be wiped out by floodwaters; there will never again be a flood to destroy the earth."

[12] And God said, "This is the sign of the covenant I am making between me and you and every living creature with you, a covenant for all future generations: [13] I have placed my bow in the clouds, and it will be a sign of the covenant between me and the earth. [14] Whenever I form clouds over the earth and the bow appears in the clouds, [15] I will remember my covenant between me and you and all the living creatures: water will never again become a flood to destroy every creature. [16] The bow will be in the clouds, and I will look at it and remember the permanent covenant between God and all the living creatures on earth." [17] God said to Noah, "This is the sign of the covenant that I have established between me and every creature on earth."

SHE READS TRUTH ◆ HE READS TRUTH

This Month's *Box*

PLAN
BEGINS

PEOPLE IN THE OLD TESTAMENT

MAY
5

GET THE MOST OUT OF YOUR SUBSCRIPTION!

**READ DAILY USING
YOUR READING GUIDE**

**FOLLOW ALONG WITH
THE COMMUNITY**

SheReadsTruth.com/app
HeReadsTruth.com/app

**LISTEN TO
WEEKLY PODCASTS**

SheReadsTruth.com/podcast

YOUR UPCOMING READING GUIDES

MAY

NAMES OF GOD

JUNE

PEOPLE IN THE
NEW TESTAMENT

JULY

PROVERBS:
WALKING IN WISDOM

RESPOND

1. WHERE DO I SEE GOD AT WORK IN NOAH'S STORY?

2. HOW DO I CONNECT TO NOAH'S EXPERIENCES? IN WHAT WAYS DO HIS EXPERIENCES FEEL FOREIGN TO ME?

3. AFTER READING NOAH'S STORY, WHAT DO I WANT TO CONTINUE TO MEDITATE ON?

ABRAHAM & SARAH

THE FATHER AND MOTHER OF GOD'S PROMISE

GENESIS 11:27–31

²⁷ These are the family records of Terah. Terah fathered Abram, Nahor, and Haran, and Haran fathered Lot. ²⁸ Haran died in his native land, in Ur of the Chaldeans, during his father Terah's lifetime. ²⁹ Abram and Nahor took wives: Abram's wife was named Sarai, and Nahor's wife was named Milcah. She was the daughter of Haran, the father of both Milcah and Iscah. ³⁰ Sarai was unable to conceive; she did not have a child.

³¹ Terah took his son Abram, his grandson Lot (Haran's son), and his daughter-in-law Sarai, his son Abram's wife, and they set out together from Ur of the Chaldeans to go to the land of Canaan. But when they came to Haran, they settled there.

GENESIS 12:1-9

THE CALL OF ABRAM

[1] The LORD said to Abram:

> Go from your land,
> your relatives,
> and your father's house
> to the land that I will show you.
> [2] I will make you into a
> great nation,
> I will bless you,
> I will make your name great,
> and you will be a blessing.
> [3] I will bless those who bless you,
> I will curse anyone who treats you
> with contempt,
> and all the peoples on earth
> will be blessed through you.

[4] So Abram went, as the LORD had told him, and Lot went with him. Abram was seventy-five years old when he left Haran. [5] He took his wife, Sarai, his nephew Lot, all the possessions they had accumulated, and the people they had acquired in Haran, and they set out for the land of Canaan. When they came to the land of Canaan, [6] Abram passed through the land to the site of Shechem, at the oak of Moreh. (At that time the Canaanites were in the land.) [7] The LORD appeared to Abram and said, "To your offspring I will give this land." So he built an altar there to the LORD who had appeared to him. [8] From there he moved on to the hill country east of Bethel and pitched his tent, with Bethel on the west and Ai on the east. He built an altar to the LORD there, and he called on the name of the LORD. [9] Then Abram journeyed by stages to the Negev.

GENESIS 15:1-21

THE ABRAHAMIC COVENANT

[1] After these events, the word of the LORD came to Abram in a vision:

> Do not be afraid, Abram.
> I am your shield;

your reward will be very great.

[2] But Abram said, "Lord GOD, what can you give me, since I am childless and the heir of my house is Eliezer of Damascus?" [3] Abram continued, "Look, you have given me no offspring, so a slave born in my house will be my heir."

[4] Now the word of the LORD came to him: "This one will not be your heir; instead, one who comes from your own body will be your heir." [5] He took him outside and said, "Look at the sky and count the stars, if you are able to count them." Then he said to him, "Your offspring will be that numerous."

[6] Abram believed the LORD, and he credited it to him as righteousness.

[7] He also said to him, "I am the LORD who brought you from Ur of the Chaldeans to give you this land to possess."

[8] But he said, "Lord GOD, how can I know that I will possess it?"

[9] He said to him, "Bring me a three-year-old cow, a three-year-old female goat, a three-year-old ram, a turtledove, and a young pigeon."

10 So he brought all these to him, cut them in half, and laid the pieces opposite each other, but he did not cut the birds in half. 11 Birds of prey came down on the carcasses, but Abram drove them away. 12 As the sun was setting, a deep sleep came over Abram, and suddenly great terror and darkness descended on him.

13 Then the LORD said to Abram, "Know this for certain: Your offspring will be resident aliens for four hundred years in a land that does not belong to them and will be enslaved and oppressed. 14 However, I will judge the nation they serve, and afterward they will go out with many possessions. 15 But you will go to your ancestors in peace and be buried at a good old age. 16 In the fourth generation they will return here, for the iniquity of the Amorites has not yet reached its full measure."

17 When the sun had set and it was dark, a smoking fire pot and a flaming torch appeared and passed between the divided animals. 18 On that day the LORD made a covenant with Abram, saying, "I give this land to your offspring, from the Brook of Egypt to the great river, the Euphrates River: 19 the land of the Kenites, Kenizzites, Kadmonites, 20 Hethites, Perizzites, Rephaim, 21 Amorites, Canaanites, Girgashites, and Jebusites."

GENESIS 18:1–15

ABRAHAM'S THREE VISITORS

1 The LORD appeared to Abraham at the oaks of Mamre while he was sitting at the entrance of his tent during the heat of the day. 2 He looked up, and he saw three men standing near him. When he saw them, he ran from the entrance of the tent to meet them, bowed to the ground, 3 and said, "My lord, if I have found favor with you, please do not go on past your servant. 4 Let a little water be brought, that you may wash your feet and rest yourselves under the tree. 5 I will bring a bit of bread so that you may strengthen yourselves. This is why you have passed your servant's way. Later, you can continue on."

"Yes," they replied, "do as you have said."

6 So Abraham hurried into the tent and said to Sarah, "Quick! Knead three measures of fine flour and make bread." 7 Abraham ran to the herd

NOTES

and got a tender, choice calf. He gave it to a young man, who hurried to prepare it. [8] Then Abraham took curds and milk, as well as the calf that he had prepared, and set them before the men. He served them as they ate under the tree.

[9] "Where is your wife Sarah?" they asked him.

"There, in the tent," he answered.

[10] The LORD said, "I will certainly come back to you in about a year's time, and your wife Sarah will have a son!" Now Sarah was listening at the entrance of the tent behind him.

[11] Abraham and Sarah were old and getting on in years. Sarah had passed the age of childbearing. [12] So she laughed to herself: "After I am worn out and my lord is old, will I have delight?"

[13] But the LORD asked Abraham, "Why did Sarah laugh, saying, 'Can I really have a baby when I'm old?' [14] Is anything impossible for the LORD? At the appointed time I will come back to you, and in about a year she will have a son."

[15] Sarah denied it. "I did not laugh," she said, because she was afraid.

But he replied, "No, you did laugh."

GENESIS 21:1-7

THE BIRTH OF ISAAC

[1] The LORD came to Sarah as he had said, and the LORD did for Sarah what he had promised. [2] Sarah became pregnant and bore a son to Abraham in his old age, at the appointed time God had told him. [3] Abraham named his son who was born to him—the one Sarah bore to him—Isaac. [4] When his son Isaac was eight days old, Abraham circumcised him, as God had commanded him. [5] Abraham was a hundred years old when his son Isaac was born to him.

[6] Sarah said, "God has made me laugh, and everyone who hears will laugh with me." [7] She also said, "Who would have told Abraham that Sarah would nurse children? Yet I have borne a son for him in his old age."

RESPOND

DATE   /   /

1. WHERE DO I SEE GOD AT WORK IN ABRAHAM AND SARAH'S STORY?

2. HOW DO I CONNECT TO ABRAHAM AND SARAH'S EXPERIENCES? IN WHAT WAYS DO THEIR EXPERIENCES FEEL FOREIGN TO ME?

3. AFTER READING ABRAHAM AND SARAH'S STORY, WHAT DO I WANT TO CONTINUE TO MEDITATE ON?

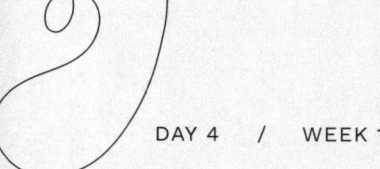

HAGAR

THE WOMAN SEEN BY GOD

GENESIS 16

HAGAR AND ISHMAEL

¹ Abram's wife, Sarai, had not borne any children for him, but she owned an Egyptian slave named Hagar. ² Sarai said to Abram, "Since the LORD has prevented me from bearing children, go to my slave; perhaps through her I can build a family." And Abram agreed to what Sarai said. ³ So Abram's wife, Sarai, took Hagar, her Egyptian slave, and gave her to her husband, Abram, as a wife for him. This happened after Abram had lived in the land of Canaan ten years. ⁴ He slept with Hagar, and she became pregnant. When she saw that she was pregnant, her mistress became contemptible to her. ⁵ Then Sarai said to Abram, "You are responsible for my suffering! I put my slave in your arms, and when she saw that she was pregnant, I became contemptible to her. May the LORD judge between me and you."

⁶ Abram replied to Sarai, "Here, your slave is in your power; do whatever you want with her." Then Sarai mistreated her so much that she ran away from her.

⁷ The angel of the LORD found her by a spring in the wilderness, the spring on the way to Shur. ⁸ He said, "Hagar, slave of Sarai, where have you come from and where are you going?"

She replied, "I'm running away from my mistress Sarai."

⁹ The angel of the LORD said to her, "Go back to your mistress and submit to her authority." ¹⁰ The angel of the LORD said to her, "I will greatly multiply your offspring, and they will be too many to count."

¹¹ The angel of the LORD said to her, "You have conceived and will have a son. You will name him Ishmael, for the LORD has heard your cry of affliction. ¹² This man will be like a wild donkey. His hand will be against everyone, and everyone's hand will be against him; he will settle near all his relatives."

¹³ So she named the LORD who spoke to her: "You are El-roi," for she said, "In this place,

have I actually seen the one who sees me?" ¹⁴ That is why the well is called Beer-lahai-roi. It is between Kadesh and Bered.

¹⁵ So Hagar gave birth to Abram's son, and Abram named his son (whom Hagar bore) Ishmael. ¹⁶ Abram was eighty-six years old when Hagar bore Ishmael to him.

GENESIS 21:8–21

HAGAR AND ISHMAEL SENT AWAY

⁸ The child grew and was weaned, and Abraham held a great feast on the day Isaac was weaned. ⁹ But Sarah saw the son mocking—the one Hagar the Egyptian had borne to Abraham. ¹⁰ So she said to Abraham, "Drive out this slave with her son, for the son of this slave will not be a coheir with my son Isaac!"

¹¹ This was very distressing to Abraham because of his son. ¹² But God said to Abraham, "Do not be distressed about the boy and about your slave. Whatever Sarah says to you, listen to her, because your offspring will be traced through Isaac, ¹³ and I will also make a nation of the slave's son because he is your offspring."

¹⁴ Early in the morning Abraham got up, took bread and a waterskin, put them on Hagar's shoulders, and sent her and the boy away. She left and wandered in the Wilderness of Beer-sheba. ¹⁵ When the water in the skin was gone, she left the boy under one of the bushes ¹⁶ and went and sat at a distance, about a bowshot away, for she said, "I can't bear to watch the boy die!" While she sat at a distance, she wept loudly.

¹⁷ God heard the boy crying, and the angel of God called to Hagar from heaven and said to her, "What's wrong, Hagar? Don't be afraid, for God has heard the boy crying from the place where he is. ¹⁸ Get up, help the boy up, and grasp his hand, for I will make him a great nation." ¹⁹ Then God opened her eyes, and she saw a well. So she went and filled the waterskin and gave the boy a drink. ²⁰ God was with the boy, and he grew; he settled in the wilderness and became an archer. ²¹ He settled in the Wilderness of Paran, and his mother got a wife for him from the land of Egypt.

RESPOND

1. WHERE DO I SEE GOD AT WORK IN HAGAR'S STORY?

2. HOW DO I CONNECT TO HAGAR'S EXPERIENCES? IN WHAT WAYS DO HER EXPERIENCES FEEL FOREIGN TO ME?

3. AFTER READING HAGAR'S STORY, WHAT DO I WANT TO CONTINUE TO MEDITATE ON?

ISAAC & REBEKAH

RECIPIENTS OF GOD'S COVENANT FAITHFULNESS

"I WILL BE WITH YOU AND BLESS YOU. FOR
I WILL GIVE ALL THESE LANDS TO YOU AND
YOUR OFFSPRING, AND I WILL CONFIRM
THE OATH THAT I SWORE TO YOUR FATHER
ABRAHAM." —GENESIS 26:3

DAY 5   WEEK 1

THE SACRIFICE OF ISAAC

¹ After these things God tested Abraham and said to him, "Abraham!"

"Here I am," he answered.

² "Take your son," he said, "your only son Isaac, whom you love, go to the land of Moriah, and offer him there as a burnt offering on one of the mountains I will tell you about."

³ So Abraham got up early in the morning, saddled his donkey, and took with him two of his young men and his son Isaac. He split wood for a burnt offering and set out to go to the place God had told him about. ⁴ On the third day Abraham looked up and saw the place in the distance. ⁵ Then Abraham said to his young men, "Stay here with the donkey. The boy and I will go over there to worship; then we'll come back to you." ⁶ Abraham took the wood for the burnt offering and laid it on his son Isaac. In his hand he took the fire and the knife, and the two of them walked on together.

⁷ Then Isaac spoke to his father Abraham and said, "My father."

And he replied, "Here I am, my son."

Isaac said, "The fire and the wood are here, but where is the lamb for the burnt offering?"

⁸ Abraham answered, "God himself will provide the lamb for the burnt offering, my son." Then the two of them walked on together.

⁹ When they arrived at the place that God had told him about, Abraham built the altar there and arranged the wood. He bound his son Isaac and placed him on the altar on top of the wood. ¹⁰ Then Abraham reached out and took the knife to slaughter his son.

¹¹ But the angel of the Lord called to him from heaven and said, "Abraham, Abraham!"

He replied, "Here I am."

¹² Then he said, "Do not lay a hand on the boy or do anything to him. For now I know that you fear God, since you have not withheld your only son from me." ¹³ Abraham looked up and saw a ram caught in the thicket by its horns. So Abraham went and took the ram and offered it as a burnt offering in place of his son. ¹⁴ And Abraham named that place The Lord Will Provide, so today it is said, "It will be provided on the Lord's mountain."

¹⁵ Then the angel of the Lord called to Abraham a second time from heaven ¹⁶ and said, "By myself I have sworn," this is the Lord's declaration: "Because you have done this thing and have not withheld your only son, ¹⁷ I will indeed bless you and make your offspring as numerous as the stars of the sky and the sand on the seashore. Your offspring will possess the city gates of their enemies. ¹⁸ And all the nations of the earth will be blessed by your offspring because you have obeyed my command."

[19] Abraham went back to his young men, and they got up and went together to Beer-sheba. And Abraham settled in Beer-sheba.

GENESIS 24:1-4, 10-27, 32-33, 42-61, 67

A WIFE FOR ISAAC

[1] Abraham was now old, getting on in years, and the LORD had blessed him in everything. [2] Abraham said to his servant, the elder of his household who managed all he owned, "Place your hand under my thigh, [3] and I will have you swear by the LORD, God of heaven and God of earth, that you will not take a wife for my son from the daughters of the Canaanites among whom I live, [4] but will go to my land and my family to take a wife for my son Isaac."

...

[10] The servant took ten of his master's camels, and with all kinds of his master's goods in hand, he went to Aram-naharaim, to Nahor's town. [11] At evening, the time when women went out to draw water, he made the camels kneel beside a well outside the town.

[12] "LORD, God of my master Abraham," he prayed, "make this happen for me today, and show kindness to my master Abraham. [13] I am standing here at the spring where the daughters of the men of the town are coming out to draw water. [14] Let the girl to whom I say, 'Please lower your water jug so that I may drink,' and who responds, 'Drink, and I'll water your camels also'—let her be the one you have appointed for your servant Isaac. By this I will know that you have shown kindness to my master."

[15] Before he had finished speaking, there was Rebekah—daughter of Bethuel son of Milcah, the wife of Abraham's brother Nahor—coming with a jug on her shoulder. [16] Now the girl was very beautiful, a virgin—no man had been intimate with her. She went down to the spring, filled her jug, and came up. [17] Then the servant ran to meet her and said, "Please let me have a little water from your jug."

[18] She replied, "Drink, my lord." She quickly lowered her jug to her hand and gave him a drink. [19] When she had finished giving him a drink, she said, "I'll also draw water for your camels until they have had enough to drink." [20] She quickly emptied her jug into the trough and hurried to the well again to draw water. She drew water for all his camels [21] while the man silently watched her to see whether or not the LORD had made his journey a success.

[22] As the camels finished drinking, the man took a gold ring weighing half a shekel, and for her wrists two bracelets weighing ten shekels of gold. [23] "Whose daughter are you?" he asked. "Please tell me, is there room in your father's house for us to spend the night?"

[24] She answered him, "I am the daughter of Bethuel son of Milcah, whom she bore to Nahor." [25] She also said to him, "We have plenty of straw and feed and a place to spend the night."

[26] Then the man knelt low, worshiped the LORD, [27] and said, "Blessed be the LORD, the God of my master Abraham, who has not withheld his kindness and faithfulness from my

master. As for me, the LORD has led me on the journey to the house of my master's relatives."

…

³² So the man came to the house, and the camels were unloaded. Straw and feed were given to the camels, and water was brought to wash his feet and the feet of the men with him.

³³ A meal was set before him, but he said, "I will not eat until I have said what I have to say."

So Laban said, "Please speak."

…

⁴² "Today when I came to the spring, I prayed: LORD, God of my master Abraham, if only you will make my journey successful! ⁴³ I am standing here at a spring. Let the young woman who comes out to draw water, and I say to her, 'Please let me drink a little water from your jug,' ⁴⁴ and who responds to me, 'Drink, and I'll draw water for your camels also'—let her be the woman the LORD has appointed for my master's son.

⁴⁵ "Before I had finished praying silently, there was Rebekah coming with her jug on her shoulder, and she went down to the spring and drew water. So I said to her, 'Please let me have a drink.' ⁴⁶ She quickly lowered her jug from her shoulder and said, 'Drink, and I'll water your camels also.' So I drank, and she also watered the camels. ⁴⁷ Then I asked her, 'Whose daughter are you?' She responded, 'The daughter of Bethuel son of Nahor, whom Milcah bore to him.' So I put the ring on her nose and the bracelets on her wrists. ⁴⁸ Then I knelt low, worshiped the LORD, and blessed the LORD, the God of my master Abraham, who guided me on the right way to take the granddaughter of my master's brother for his son. ⁴⁹ Now, if you are going to show kindness and faithfulness to my master, tell me; if not, tell me, and I will go elsewhere."

⁵⁰ Laban and Bethuel answered, "This is from the LORD; we have no choice in the matter. ⁵¹ Rebekah is here in front of you. Take her and go, and let her be a wife for your master's son, just as the LORD has spoken."

⁵² When Abraham's servant heard their words, he bowed to the ground before the Lord. ⁵³ Then he brought out objects of silver and gold, and garments, and gave them to Rebekah. He also gave precious gifts to her brother and her mother. ⁵⁴ Then he and the men with him ate and drank and spent the night.

When they got up in the morning, he said, "Send me to my master."

⁵⁵ But her brother and mother said, "Let the girl stay with us for about ten days. Then she can go."

⁵⁶ But he responded to them, "Do not delay me, since the Lord has made my journey a success. Send me away so that I may go to my master."

⁵⁷ So they said, "Let's call the girl and ask her opinion."

⁵⁸ They called Rebekah and said to her, "Will you go with this man?"

She replied, "I will go." ⁵⁹ So they sent away their sister Rebekah with the one who had nursed and raised her, and Abraham's servant and his men.

⁶⁰ They blessed Rebekah, saying to her:

Our sister, may you become
thousands upon ten thousands.
May your offspring possess
the city gates of their enemies.

⁶¹ Then Rebekah and her female servants got up, mounted the camels, and followed the man. So the servant took Rebekah and left.

…

⁶⁷ And Isaac brought her into the tent of his mother Sarah and took Rebekah to be his wife. Isaac loved her, and he was comforted after his mother's death.

GENESIS 26:1–6

THE PROMISE REAFFIRMED TO ISAAC

¹ There was another famine in the land in addition to the one that had occurred in Abraham's time. And Isaac went to Abimelech, king of the Philistines, at Gerar. ² The Lord appeared to him and said, "Do not go down to Egypt. Live in the land that I tell you about; ³ stay in this land as an alien, and I will be with you and bless you. For I will give all these lands to you and your offspring, and

I WILL CONFIRM THE OATH THAT I SWORE TO YOUR FATHER ABRAHAM.

⁴ I will make your offspring as numerous as the stars of the sky, I will give your offspring all these lands, and all the nations of the earth will be blessed by your offspring, ⁵ because Abraham listened to me and kept my mandate, my commands, my statutes, and my instructions." ⁶ So Isaac settled in Gerar.

RESPOND

1. WHERE DO I SEE GOD AT WORK IN ISAAC AND REBEKAH'S STORY?

2. HOW DO I CONNECT TO ISAAC AND REBEKAH'S EXPERIENCES? IN WHAT WAYS DO THEIR EXPERIENCES FEEL FOREIGN TO ME?

3. AFTER READING ISAAC AND REBEKAH'S STORY, WHAT DO I WANT TO CONTINUE TO MEDITATE ON?

GRACE DAY

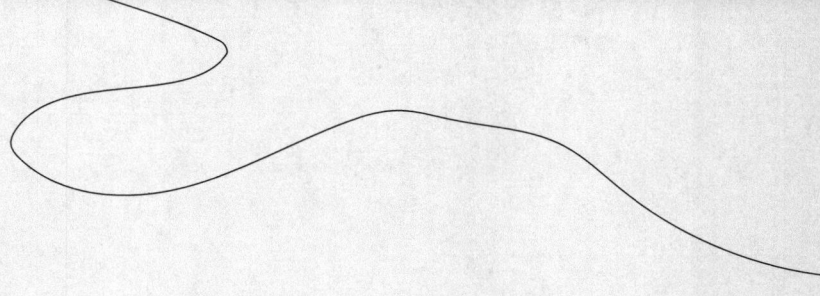

TAKE THIS DAY TO CATCH UP ON
YOUR READING, PRAY, AND REST IN
THE PRESENCE OF THE LORD.

FOR YOU ARE SAVED BY GRACE
THROUGH FAITH, AND THIS IS NOT
FROM YOURSELVES; IT IS GOD'S
GIFT—NOT FROM WORKS, SO THAT
NO ONE CAN BOAST. FOR WE ARE HIS
WORKMANSHIP, CREATED IN CHRIST
JESUS FOR GOOD WORKS, WHICH
GOD PREPARED AHEAD OF TIME FOR
US TO DO.

EPHESIANS 2:8–10

WEEKLY

SCRIPTURE IS GOD BREATHED AND TRUE. WHEN
WE MEMORIZE IT, WE CARRY THE GOOD NEWS
OF JESUS WITH US WHEREVER WE GO.

FOR THIS PLAN, WE WILL MEMORIZE OUR KEY
PASSAGE, PSALM 8:3–4. WE WILL BEGIN WITH
THE FIRST LINE.

SEE TIPS FOR MEMORIZING SCRIPTURE ON PAGE 236.

7 # TRUTH

PSALM 8:3–4

WHEN I OBSERVE YOUR HEAVENS,
THE WORK OF YOUR FINGERS,
THE MOON AND THE STARS,
WHICH YOU SET IN PLACE,
WHAT IS A HUMAN BEING THAT YOU REMEMBER HIM,
A SON OF MAN THAT YOU LOOK AFTER HIM?

JACOB

THE MAN WHO WAS RENAMED ISRAEL

GENESIS 25:19–26

THE BIRTH OF JACOB AND ESAU

¹⁹ These are the family records of Isaac son of Abraham. Abraham fathered Isaac. ²⁰ Isaac was forty years old when he took as his wife Rebekah daughter of Bethuel the Aramean from Paddan-aram and sister of Laban the Aramean. ²¹ Isaac prayed to the Lord on behalf of his wife because she was childless. The Lord was receptive to his prayer, and his wife Rebekah conceived. ²² But the children inside her struggled with each other, and she said, "Why is this happening to me?" So she went to inquire of the Lord. ²³ And the Lord said to her:

> Two nations are in your womb;
> two peoples will come from you and be separated.
> One people will be stronger than the other,
> and the older will serve the younger.

²⁴ When her time came to give birth, there were indeed twins in her womb. ²⁵ The first one came out red-looking, covered with hair like a fur coat, and they named him Esau. ²⁶ After this, his brother came out grasping Esau's heel with his hand. So he was named Jacob. Isaac was sixty years old when they were born.

GENESIS 28:10-22

JACOB AT BETHEL

¹⁰ Jacob left Beer-sheba and went toward Haran. ¹¹ He reached a certain place and spent the night there because the sun had set. He took one of the stones from the place, put it there at his head, and lay down in that place. ¹² And he dreamed: A stairway was set on the ground with its top reaching the sky, and God's angels were going up and down on it. ¹³ The LORD was standing there beside him, saying, "I am the LORD, the God of your father Abraham and the God of Isaac. I will give you and your offspring the land on which you are lying. ¹⁴ Your offspring will be like the dust of the earth, and you will spread out toward the west, the east, the north, and the south. All the peoples on earth will be blessed through you and your offspring. ¹⁵ Look, I am with you and will watch over you wherever you go. I will bring you back to this land, for I will not leave you until I have done what I have promised you."

¹⁶ When Jacob awoke from his sleep, he said, "Surely the LORD is in this place, and I did not know it." ¹⁷ He was afraid and said, "What an awesome place this is! This is none other than the house of God. This is the gate of heaven."

¹⁸ Early in the morning Jacob took the stone that was near his head and set it up as a marker. He poured oil on top of it ¹⁹ and named the place Bethel, though previously the city was named Luz. ²⁰ Then Jacob made a vow: "If God will be with me and watch over me during this journey I'm making, if he provides me with food to eat and clothing to wear, ²¹ and if I return safely to my father's family, then the LORD will be my God. ²² This stone that I have set up as a marker will be God's house, and I will give to you a tenth of all that you give me."

GENESIS 31:13

"I am the God of Bethel, where you poured oil on the stone marker and made a solemn vow to me. Get up, leave this land, and return to your native land."

GENESIS 32:3-32

³ Jacob sent messengers ahead of him to his brother Esau in the land of Seir, the territory of Edom. ⁴ He commanded them, "You are to say to my lord Esau, 'This is what your servant Jacob says. I have been staying with Laban and have been delayed until now. ⁵ I have oxen, donkeys, flocks, and male and female slaves. I have sent this message to inform my lord, in order to seek your favor.'"

⁶ When the messengers returned to Jacob, they said, "We went to your brother Esau; he is coming to meet you—and he has four hundred men with him." ⁷ Jacob was greatly afraid and distressed; he divided the people with him into two camps, along with the flocks, herds, and camels. ⁸ He thought, "If Esau comes to one camp and attacks it, the remaining one can escape."

⁹ Then Jacob said, "God of my father Abraham and God of my father Isaac, the LORD who said to me, 'Go back to your land and to your family, and I will cause you to prosper,' ¹⁰ I am unworthy of all the kindness and faithfulness you have shown your servant. Indeed, I crossed over the Jordan with my staff, and now I have become two camps. ¹¹ Please rescue me from my brother Esau, for I am afraid of him; otherwise, he may come and attack me, the mothers, and their children. ¹² You have said, 'I will cause you to prosper, and I will make your offspring like the sand of the sea, too numerous to be counted.'"

[13] He spent the night there and took part of what he had brought with him as a gift for his brother Esau: [14] two hundred female goats, twenty male goats, two hundred ewes, twenty rams, [15] thirty milk camels with their young, forty cows, ten bulls, twenty female donkeys, and ten male donkeys. [16] He entrusted them to his slaves as separate herds and said to them, "Go on ahead of me, and leave some distance between the herds."

[17] And he told the first one, "When my brother Esau meets you and asks, 'Who do you belong to? Where are you going? And whose animals are these ahead of you?' [18] then tell him, 'They belong to your servant Jacob. They are a gift sent to my lord Esau. And look, he is behind us.'"

[19] He also told the second one, the third, and everyone who was walking behind the animals, "Say the same thing to Esau when you find him. [20] You are also to say, 'Look, your servant Jacob is right behind us.'" For he thought, "I want to appease Esau with the gift that is going ahead of me. After that, I can face him, and perhaps he will forgive me."

[21] So the gift was sent on ahead of him while he remained in the camp that night. [22] During the night Jacob got up and took his two wives, his two slave women, and his eleven sons, and crossed the ford of Jabbok. [23] He took them and sent them across the stream, along with all his possessions.

JACOB WRESTLES WITH GOD

[24] Jacob was left alone, and a man wrestled with him until daybreak. [25] When the man saw that he could not defeat him, he struck Jacob's hip socket as they wrestled and dislocated his hip. [26] Then he said to Jacob, "Let me go, for it is daybreak."

But Jacob said, "I will not let you go unless you bless me."

[27] "What is your name?" the man asked.

"Jacob," he replied.

[28] "Your name will no longer be Jacob," he said. "It will be Israel because you have struggled with God and with men and have prevailed."

[29] Then Jacob asked him, "Please tell me your name."

But he answered, "Why do you ask my name?" And he blessed him there.

[30] Jacob then named the place Peniel, "For I have seen God face to face," he said, "yet my life has been spared." [31] The sun shone on him as he passed by Penuel—limping because of his hip. [32] That is why, still today, the Israelites don't eat the thigh muscle that is at the hip socket: because he struck Jacob's hip socket at the thigh muscle.

GENESIS 35:9-15

[9] God appeared to Jacob again after he returned from Paddan-aram, and he blessed him. [10] God said to him, "Your name is Jacob; you will no longer be named Jacob, but your name will be Israel." So he named him Israel. [11] God also said to him, "I am God Almighty. Be fruitful and multiply.

A NATION, INDEED AN ASSEMBLY OF NATIONS, WILL COME FROM YOU, AND KINGS WILL DESCEND FROM YOU.

[12] I will give to you the land that I gave to Abraham and Isaac. And I will give the land to your future descendants." [13] Then God withdrew from him at the place where he had spoken to him.

[14] Jacob set up a marker at the place where he had spoken to him—a stone marker. He poured a drink offering on it and poured oil on it. [15] Jacob named the place where God had spoken with him Bethel.

RESPOND

01 WHERE DO I SEE GOD AT WORK IN
JACOB'S STORY?

_____

_____

_____

_____

_____

_____

_____

_____

_____

02 HOW DO I CONNECT TO JACOB'S
EXPERIENCES? IN WHAT WAYS DO HIS
EXPERIENCES FEEL FOREIGN TO ME?

_____

_____

_____

_____

_____

_____

_____

_____

_____

03 AFTER READING JACOB'S STORY, WHAT DO I WANT TO CONTINUE TO MEDITATE ON?

_____

_____

_____

_____

_____

_____

_____

_____

JOSEPH

DAY 9 ———————— WEEK 2

GENESIS 37:1–13, 18–28

JOSEPH'S DREAMS

¹ Jacob lived in the land where his father had stayed, the land of Canaan. ² These are the family records of Jacob.

At seventeen years of age, Joseph tended sheep with his brothers. The young man was working with the sons of Bilhah and Zilpah, his father's wives, and he brought a bad report about them to their father.

³ Now Israel loved Joseph more than his other sons because Joseph was a son born to him in his old age, and he made a long-sleeved robe for him. ⁴ When his brothers saw that their father loved him more than all his brothers, they hated him and could not bring themselves to speak peaceably to him.

⁵ Then Joseph had a dream. When he told it to his brothers, they hated him even more. ⁶ He said to them, "Listen to this dream I had: ⁷ There we were, binding sheaves of grain in the field. Suddenly my sheaf stood up, and your sheaves gathered around it and bowed down to my sheaf."

⁸ "Are you really going to reign over us?" his brothers asked him. "Are you really going to

rule us?" So they hated him even more because of his dream and what he had said.

⁹ Then he had another dream and told it to his brothers. "Look," he said, "I had another dream, and this time the sun, moon, and eleven stars were bowing down to me."

¹⁰ He told his father and brothers, and his father rebuked him. "What kind of dream is this that you have had?" he said. "Am I and your mother and your brothers really going to come and bow down to the ground before you?" ¹¹ His brothers were jealous of him, but his father kept the matter in mind.

JOSEPH SOLD INTO SLAVERY

¹² His brothers had gone to pasture their father's flocks at Shechem. ¹³ Israel said to Joseph, "Your brothers, you know, are pasturing the flocks at Shechem. Get ready. I'm sending you to them."

"I'm ready," Joseph replied.

…

¹⁸ They saw him in the distance, and before he had reached them, they plotted to kill him.

¹⁹ They said to one another, "Oh, look, here comes that dream expert! ²⁰ So now, come on, let's kill him and throw him into one of the pits. We can say that a vicious animal ate him. Then we'll see what becomes of his dreams!"

²¹ When Reuben heard this, he tried to save him from them. He said, "Let's not take his life." ²² Reuben also said to them, "Don't shed blood. Throw him into this pit in the wilderness, but don't lay a hand on him"—intending to rescue him from them and return him to his father.

²³ When Joseph came to his brothers, they stripped off Joseph's robe, the long-sleeved robe that he had on. ²⁴ Then they took him and threw him into the pit. The pit was empty, without water.

²⁵ They sat down to eat a meal, and when they looked up, there was a caravan of Ishmaelites coming from Gilead. Their camels were carrying aromatic gum, balsam, and resin, going down to Egypt.

²⁶ Judah said to his brothers, "What do we gain if we kill our brother and cover up his blood? ²⁷ Come on, let's sell him to the Ishmaelites and not lay a hand on him, for he is our brother, our own flesh," and his brothers agreed. ²⁸ When Midianite traders passed by, his brothers pulled Joseph out of the pit and sold him for twenty pieces of silver to the Ishmaelites, who took Joseph to Egypt.

GENESIS 39:21-23

JOSEPH IN PRISON

²¹ But the LORD was with Joseph and extended kindness to him. He granted him favor with the prison warden. ²² The warden put all the prisoners who were in the prison under Joseph's authority, and he was responsible for everything that was done there. ²³ The warden did not bother with anything under Joseph's authority, because the LORD was with him, and the LORD made everything that he did successful.

GENESIS 41:46-57

JOSEPH'S ADMINISTRATION

⁴⁶ Joseph was thirty years old when he entered the service of Pharaoh king of Egypt. Joseph left Pharaoh's presence and traveled throughout the land of Egypt.

47 During the seven years of abundance the land produced outstanding harvests. 48 Joseph gathered all the excess food in the land of Egypt during the seven years and put it in the cities. He put the food in every city from the fields around it. 49 So Joseph stored up grain in such abundance—like the sand of the sea—that he stopped measuring it because it was beyond measure.

50 Two sons were born to Joseph before the years of famine arrived. Asenath daughter of Potiphera, priest at On, bore them to him. 51 Joseph named the firstborn Manasseh and said, "God has made me forget all my hardship and my whole family." 52 And the second son he named Ephraim and said, "God has made me fruitful in the land of my affliction."

53 Then the seven years of abundance in the land of Egypt came to an end, 54 and the seven years of famine began, just as Joseph had said. There was famine in every land, but in the whole land of Egypt there was food. 55 When the whole land of Egypt was stricken with famine, the people cried out to Pharaoh for food. Pharaoh told all Egypt, "Go to Joseph and do whatever he tells you." 56 Now the famine had spread across the whole region, so Joseph opened all the storehouses and sold grain to the Egyptians,

for the famine was severe in the land of Egypt. 57 Every land came to Joseph in Egypt to buy grain, for the famine was severe in every land.

GENESIS 50:15-21

JOSEPH'S KINDNESS

15 When Joseph's brothers saw that their father was dead, they said to one another, "If Joseph is holding a grudge against us, he will certainly repay us for all the suffering we caused him."

16 So they sent this message to Joseph, "Before he died your father gave a command: 17 'Say this to Joseph: Please forgive your brothers' transgression and their sin—the suffering they caused you.' Therefore, please forgive the transgression of the servants of the God of your father." Joseph wept when their message came to him. 18 His brothers also came to him, bowed down before him, and said, "We are your slaves!"

19 But Joseph said to them, "Don't be afraid. Am I in the place of God? 20 You planned evil against me; God planned it for good to bring about the present result—the survival of many people. 21 Therefore don't be afraid. I will take care of you and your children." And he comforted them and spoke kindly to them.

RESPOND

DATE   /   /

01 WHERE DO I SEE GOD AT WORK IN
JOSEPH'S STORY?

_____
_____
_____
_____
_____
_____
_____
_____
_____

02 HOW DO I CONNECT TO JOSEPH'S
EXPERIENCES? IN WHAT WAYS DO HIS
EXPERIENCES FEEL FOREIGN TO ME?

_____
_____
_____
_____
_____
_____
_____
_____
_____

03 AFTER READING JOSEPH'S STORY, WHAT DO I WANT TO CONTINUE TO MEDITATE ON?

_____
_____
_____
_____
_____
_____
_____
_____
_____

SHIPHRAH & PUAH

THE MIDWIVES WHO FEARED GOD

EXODUS 1:6–21

[6] Joseph and all his brothers and all that generation eventually died. [7] But the Israelites were fruitful, increased rapidly, multiplied, and became extremely numerous so that the land was filled with them.

[8] A new king, who did not know about Joseph, came to power in Egypt. [9] He said to his people, "Look, the Israelite people are more numerous and powerful than we are. [10] Come, let's deal shrewdly with them; otherwise they will multiply further, and when war breaks out, they will join our enemies, fight against us, and leave the country." [11] So the Egyptians assigned taskmasters over the Israelites to oppress them with forced labor. They built Pithom and Rameses as supply cities for Pharaoh. [12] But the more they oppressed them, the more they multiplied and spread so that the Egyptians came to dread the Israelites. [13] They worked

the Israelites ruthlessly [14] and made their lives bitter with difficult labor in brick and mortar and in all kinds of fieldwork. They ruthlessly imposed all this work on them.

[15] The king of Egypt said to the Hebrew midwives—the first, whose name was Shiphrah, and the second, whose name was Puah— [16] "When you help the Hebrew women give birth, observe them as they deliver. If the child is a son, kill him, but if it's a daughter, she may live." [17] The midwives, however, feared God and did not do as the king of Egypt had told them; they let the boys live. [18] So the king of Egypt summoned the midwives and asked them, "Why have you done this and let the boys live?"

[19] The midwives said to Pharaoh, "The Hebrew women are not like the Egyptian women, for they are vigorous and give birth before the midwife can get to them."

[20] SO GOD WAS GOOD TO THE MIDWIVES, AND THE PEOPLE MULTIPLIED AND BECAME VERY NUMEROUS.

[21] Since the midwives feared God, he gave them families.

RESPOND

01 WHERE DO I SEE GOD AT WORK IN SHIPHRAH AND PUAH'S STORY?

_____
_____
_____
_____
_____
_____
_____
_____
_____
_____

02 HOW DO I CONNECT TO SHIPHRAH AND PUAH'S EXPERIENCES? IN WHAT WAYS DO THEIR EXPERIENCES FEEL FOREIGN TO ME?

_____
_____
_____
_____
_____
_____
_____
_____
_____
_____

03 AFTER READING SHIPHRAH AND PUAH'S STORY, WHAT DO I WANT TO CONTINUE TO MEDITATE ON?

_____
_____
_____
_____
_____
_____
_____
_____
_____

MOSES

A LEADER FOR GOD'S PEOPLE

PEOPLE IN THE OLD TESTAMENT

EXODUS 3

MOSES AND THE BURNING BUSH

¹ Meanwhile, Moses was shepherding the flock of his father-in-law Jethro, the priest of Midian. He led the flock to the far side of the wilderness and came to Horeb, the mountain of God. ² Then the angel of the LORD appeared to him in a flame of fire within a bush. As Moses looked, he saw that the bush was on fire but was not consumed. ³ So Moses thought, "I must go over and look at this remarkable sight. Why isn't the bush burning up?"

⁴ When the LORD saw that he had gone over to look, God called out to him from the bush, "Moses, Moses!"

"Here I am," he answered.

⁵ "Do not come closer," he said. "Remove the sandals from your feet, for the place where you are standing is holy ground." ⁶ Then he continued, "I am the God of your father, the God of Abraham, the God of Isaac, and the God of Jacob." Moses hid his face because he was afraid to look at God.

⁷ Then the LORD said, "I have observed the misery of my people in Egypt, and have heard them crying out because of their oppressors. I know about their sufferings, ⁸ and I have come down to rescue them from the power of the Egyptians and to bring them from that land to a good and spacious land, a land flowing with milk and honey—the territory of the Canaanites, Hethites, Amorites, Perizzites, Hivites, and Jebusites. ⁹ So because the Israelites' cry for help has come to me, and I have also seen the way the Egyptians are oppressing them, ¹⁰ therefore, go. I am sending you to Pharaoh so that you may lead my people, the Israelites, out of Egypt."

¹¹ But Moses asked God, "Who am I that I should go to Pharaoh and that I should bring the Israelites out of Egypt?"

¹² He answered, "I will certainly be with you, and this will be the sign to you that I am the one who sent you: when you bring the people out of Egypt, you will all worship God at this mountain."

[13] Then Moses asked God, "If I go to the Israelites and say to them, 'The God of your ancestors has sent me to you,' and they ask me, 'What is his name?' what should I tell them?"

[14] God replied to Moses, "I AM WHO I AM. This is what you are to say to the Israelites: I AM has sent me to you." [15] God also said to Moses, "Say this to the Israelites: The LORD, the God of your ancestors, the God of Abraham, the God of Isaac, and the God of Jacob, has sent me to you. This is my name forever; this is how I am to be remembered in every generation.

[16] "Go and assemble the elders of Israel and say to them: The LORD, the God of your ancestors, the God of Abraham, Isaac, and Jacob, has appeared to me and said: I have paid close attention to you and to what has been done to you in Egypt. [17] And I have promised you that I will bring you up from the misery of Egypt to the land of the Canaanites, Hethites, Amorites, Perizzites, Hivites, and Jebusites—a land flowing with milk and honey. [18] They will listen to what you say. Then you, along with the elders of Israel, must go to the king of Egypt and say to him: The LORD, the God of the Hebrews, has met with us. Now please let us go on a three-day trip into the wilderness so that we may sacrifice to the LORD our God.

[19] "However, I know that the king of Egypt will not allow you to go, even under force from a strong hand. [20] But when I stretch out my hand and strike Egypt with all my miracles that I will perform in it, after that, he will let you go. [21] And I will give these people such favor with the Egyptians that when you go, you will not go empty-handed. [22] Each woman will ask her neighbor and any woman staying in her house for silver and gold jewelry, and clothing, and you will put them on your sons and daughters. So you will plunder the Egyptians."

EXODUS 13:17-22

THE ROUTE OF THE EXODUS

[17] When Pharaoh let the people go, God did not lead them along the road to the land of the Philistines, even though it was nearby; for God said, "The people will change their minds and return to Egypt if they face war." [18] So he led the people around toward the Red Sea along the road of the wilderness. And the Israelites left the land of Egypt in battle formation.

¹⁹ Moses took the bones of Joseph with him, because Joseph had made the Israelites swear a solemn oath, saying, "God will certainly come to your aid; then you must take my bones with you from this place."

²⁰ They set out from Succoth and camped at Etham on the edge of the wilderness. ²¹ The LORD went ahead of them in a pillar of cloud to lead them on their way during the day and in a pillar of fire to give them light at night, so that they could travel day or night. ²² The pillar of cloud by day and the pillar of fire by night never left its place in front of the people.

EXODUS 19:1–6

ISRAEL AT SINAI

¹ In the third month from the very day the Israelites left the land of Egypt, they came to the Sinai Wilderness. ² They traveled from Rephidim, came to the Sinai Wilderness, and camped in the wilderness. Israel camped there in front of the mountain.

³ MOSES WENT UP THE MOUNTAIN TO GOD, AND THE LORD CALLED TO HIM FROM THE MOUNTAIN: "THIS IS WHAT YOU MUST SAY TO THE HOUSE OF JACOB AND EXPLAIN TO THE ISRAELITES:

⁴ 'You have seen what I did to the Egyptians and how I carried you on eagles' wings and brought you to myself. ⁵ Now if you will carefully listen to me and keep my covenant, you will be my own possession out of all the peoples, although the whole earth is mine, ⁶ and you will be my kingdom of priests and my holy nation.' These are the words that you are to say to the Israelites."

EXODUS 33:7–23

⁷ Now Moses took a tent and pitched it outside the camp, at a distance from the camp; he called it the tent of meeting. Anyone who wanted to consult the LORD would go to the tent of meeting that was outside the camp. ⁸ Whenever Moses went out to the tent, all the people would stand up, each one at the door of his tent, and they would watch Moses until he entered the tent. ⁹ When Moses entered the tent, the pillar of cloud would come down and remain at the entrance to the tent, and the

LORD would speak with Moses. [10] As all the people saw the pillar of cloud remaining at the entrance to the tent, they would stand up, then bow in worship, each one at the door of his tent. [11] The LORD would speak with Moses face to face, just as a man speaks with his friend, then Moses would return to the camp. His assistant, the young man Joshua son of Nun, would not leave the inside of the tent.

THE LORD'S GLORY

[12] Moses said to the LORD, "Look, you have told me, 'Lead this people up,' but you have not let me know whom you will send with me. You said, 'I know you by name, and you have also found favor with me.' [13] Now if I have indeed found favor with you, please teach me your ways, and I will know you, so that I may find favor with you. Now consider that this nation is your people."

[14] And he replied, "My presence will go with you, and I will give you rest."

[15] "If your presence does not go," Moses responded to him, "don't make us go up from here. [16] How will it be known that I and your people have found favor with you unless you go with us? I and your people will be distinguished by this from all the other people on the face of the earth."

[17] The LORD answered Moses, "I will do this very thing you have asked, for you have found favor with me, and I know you by name."

[18] Then Moses said, "Please, let me see your glory."

[19] He said, "I will cause all my goodness to pass in front of you, and I will proclaim the name 'the LORD' before you. I will be gracious to whom I will be gracious, and I will have compassion on whom I will have compassion." [20] But he added, "You cannot see my face, for humans cannot see me and live." [21] The LORD said, "Here is a place near me. You are to stand on the rock, [22] and when my glory passes by, I will put you in the crevice of the rock and cover you with my hand until I have passed by. [23] Then I will take my hand away, and you will see my back, but my face will not be seen."

RESPOND

DATE   /   /

01 WHERE DO I SEE GOD AT WORK IN
MOSES'S STORY?

_____

_____

_____

_____

_____

_____

_____

_____

_____

_____

02 HOW DO I CONNECT TO MOSES'S
EXPERIENCES? IN WHAT WAYS DO HIS
EXPERIENCES FEEL FOREIGN TO ME?

_____

_____

_____

_____

_____

_____

_____

_____

_____

_____

_____

03 AFTER READING MOSES'S STORY, WHAT DO I WANT TO CONTINUE TO MEDITATE ON?

_____

_____

_____

_____

_____

_____

_____

_____

_____

MIRIAM

A PROPHETESS WITH PRAISE ON HER LIPS

THE PROPHETESS MIRIAM, AARON'S SISTER,
TOOK A TAMBOURINE IN HER HAND, AND ALL
THE WOMEN CAME OUT FOLLOWING HER WITH
TAMBOURINES AND DANCING. —EXODUS 15:20

DAY 12   WEEK 2

MOSES'S BIRTH AND ADOPTION

¹ Now a man from the family of Levi married a Levite woman. ² The woman became pregnant and gave birth to a son; when she saw that he was beautiful, she hid him for three months. ³ But when she could no longer hide him, she got a papyrus basket for him and coated it with asphalt and pitch. She placed the child in it and set it among the reeds by the bank of the Nile.

⁴ THEN HIS SISTER STOOD AT A DISTANCE IN ORDER TO SEE WHAT WOULD HAPPEN TO HIM.

⁵ Pharaoh's daughter went down to bathe at the Nile while her servant girls walked along the riverbank. She saw the basket among the reeds, sent her slave girl, took it, ⁶ opened it, and saw him, the child—and there he was, a little boy, crying. She felt sorry for him and said, "This is one of the Hebrew boys."

⁷ Then his sister said to Pharaoh's daughter, "Should I go and call a Hebrew woman who is nursing to nurse the boy for you?"

⁸ "Go," Pharaoh's daughter told her. So the girl went and called the boy's mother.

EXODUS 14

¹ Then the LORD spoke to Moses: ² "Tell the Israelites to turn back and camp in front of Pi-hahiroth, between Migdol and the sea; you must camp in front of Baal-zephon, facing it by the sea. ³ Pharaoh will say of the Israelites: They are wandering around the land in confusion; the wilderness has boxed them in. ⁴ I will harden Pharaoh's heart so that he will pursue them. Then I will receive glory by means of Pharaoh and all his army, and the Egyptians will know that I am the LORD." So the Israelites did this.

THE EGYPTIAN PURSUIT

[5] When the king of Egypt was told that the people had fled, Pharaoh and his officials changed their minds about the people and said, "What have we done? We have released Israel from serving us." [6] So he got his chariot ready and took his troops with him; [7] he took six hundred of the best chariots and all the rest of the chariots of Egypt, with officers in each one. [8] The LORD hardened the heart of Pharaoh king of Egypt, and he pursued the Israelites, who were going out defiantly. [9] The Egyptians—all Pharaoh's horses and chariots, his horsemen, and his army—chased after them and caught up with them as they camped by the sea beside Pi-hahiroth, in front of Baal-zephon.

[10] As Pharaoh approached, the Israelites looked up and there were the Egyptians coming after them! The Israelites were terrified and cried out to the LORD for help. [11] They said to Moses, "Is it because there are no graves in Egypt that you have taken us away to die in the wilderness? What have you done to us by bringing us out of Egypt? [12] Isn't this what we told you in Egypt: Leave us alone so that we may serve the Egyptians? It would have been better for us to serve the Egyptians than to die in the wilderness."

[13] But Moses said to the people, "Don't be afraid.

STAND FIRM AND SEE THE LORD'S SALVATION THAT HE WILL ACCOMPLISH FOR YOU TODAY;

for the Egyptians you see today, you will never see again. [14] The LORD will fight for you, and you must be quiet."

ESCAPE THROUGH THE RED SEA

[15] The LORD said to Moses, "Why are you crying out to me? Tell the Israelites to break camp. [16] As for you, lift up your staff, stretch out your hand over the sea, and divide it so that the Israelites can go through the sea on dry ground. [17] As for me, I am going to harden the hearts of the Egyptians so that they will go in after them, and I will receive glory by means of Pharaoh, all his army, and his chariots and horsemen. [18] The Egyptians will know that I am the LORD when I receive glory through Pharaoh, his chariots, and his horsemen."

¹⁹ Then the angel of God, who was going in front of the Israelite forces, moved and went behind them. The pillar of cloud moved from in front of them and stood behind them. ²⁰ It came between the Egyptian and Israelite forces. There was cloud and darkness, it lit up the night, and neither group came near the other all night long.

²¹ Then Moses stretched out his hand over the sea. The LORD drove the sea back with a powerful east wind all that night and turned the sea into dry land. So the waters were divided, ²² and the Israelites went through the sea on dry ground, with the waters like a wall to them on their right and their left.

²³ The Egyptians set out in pursuit—all Pharaoh's horses, his chariots, and his horsemen—and went into the sea after them. ²⁴ During the morning watch, the LORD looked down at the Egyptian forces from the pillar of fire and cloud, and threw the Egyptian forces into confusion. ²⁵ He caused their chariot wheels to swerve and made them drive with difficulty. "Let's get away from Israel," the Egyptians said, "because the LORD is fighting for them against Egypt!"

²⁶ Then the LORD said to Moses, "Stretch out your hand over the sea so that the water may come back on the Egyptians, on their chariots and horsemen." ²⁷ So Moses stretched out his hand over the sea, and at daybreak the sea returned to its normal depth. While the Egyptians were trying to escape from it, the LORD threw them into the sea. ²⁸ The water came back and covered the chariots and horsemen, plus the entire army of Pharaoh that had gone after them into the sea. Not even one of them survived.

²⁹ But the Israelites had walked through the sea on dry ground, with the waters like a wall to them on their right and their left. ³⁰ That day the LORD saved Israel from the power of the Egyptians, and Israel saw the Egyptians dead on the seashore. ³¹ When Israel saw the great power that the LORD used against the Egyptians, the people feared the LORD and believed in him and in his servant Moses.

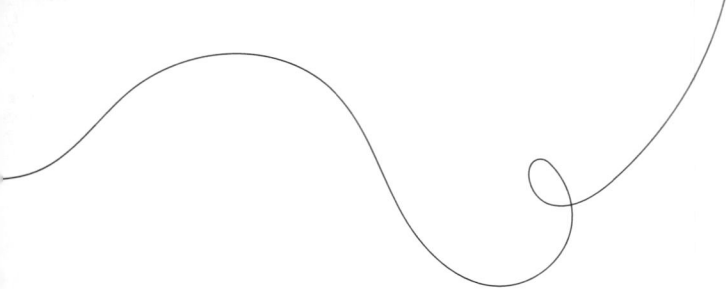

EXODUS 15:19–21

[19] When Pharaoh's horses with his chariots and horsemen went into the sea, the LORD brought the water of the sea back over them. But the Israelites walked through the sea on dry ground. [20] Then the prophetess Miriam, Aaron's sister, took a tambourine in her hand, and all the women came out following her with tambourines and dancing. [21] Miriam sang to them:

> Sing to the LORD,
> for he is highly exalted;
> he has thrown the horse
> and its rider into the sea.

RESPOND

DATE   /   /

01 WHERE DO I SEE GOD AT WORK IN
MIRIAM'S STORY?

_____
_____
_____
_____
_____
_____
_____
_____
_____
_____

02 HOW DO I CONNECT TO MIRIAM'S
EXPERIENCES? IN WHAT WAYS DO HER
EXPERIENCES FEEL FOREIGN TO ME?

_____
_____
_____
_____
_____
_____
_____
_____
_____
_____

03 AFTER READING MIRIAM'S STORY, WHAT DO I WANT TO CONTINUE TO MEDITATE ON?

_____
_____
_____
_____
_____
_____
_____
_____
_____
_____

GRACE DAY

TAKE THIS DAY TO CATCH UP ON
YOUR READING, PRAY, AND REST IN
THE PRESENCE OF THE LORD.

SEE WHAT GREAT LOVE THE FATHER
HAS GIVEN US THAT WE SHOULD BE
CALLED GOD'S CHILDREN—AND WE
ARE! THE REASON THE WORLD DOES
NOT KNOW US IS THAT IT DIDN'T
KNOW HIM.

1 JOHN 3:1

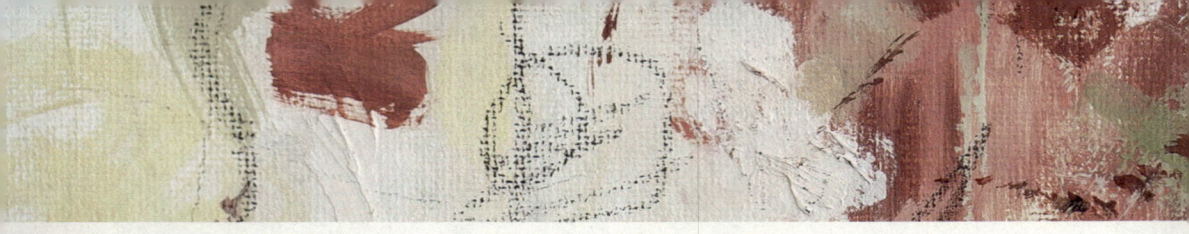

WEEKLY

DAY

SCRIPTURE IS GOD BREATHED AND TRUE. WHEN WE MEMORIZE IT, WE CARRY THE GOOD NEWS OF JESUS WITH US WHEREVER WE GO.

FOR THIS PLAN, WE ARE MEMORIZING OUR KEY PASSAGE, PSALM 8:3–4. WE WILL CONTINUE WITH THE SECOND LINE.

SEE TIPS FOR MEMORIZING SCRIPTURE ON PAGE 236.

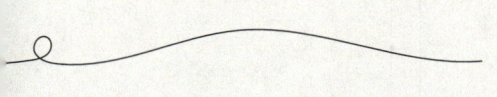

14   TRUTH

PSALM 8:3–4

WHEN I OBSERVE YOUR HEAVENS,
THE WORK OF YOUR FINGERS,
THE MOON AND THE STARS,
WHICH YOU SET IN PLACE,
WHAT IS A HUMAN BEING THAT YOU REMEMBER HIM,
A SON OF MAN THAT YOU LOOK AFTER HIM?

AARON

EXODUS 4:13-17, 27-31

¹³ Moses said, "Please, Lord, send someone else."

¹⁴ Then the LORD's anger burned against Moses, and he said, "Isn't Aaron the Levite your brother? I know that he can speak well. And also, he is on his way now to meet you. He will rejoice when he sees you. ¹⁵ You will speak with him and tell him what to say. I will help both you and him to speak and will teach you both what to do. ¹⁶ He will speak to the people for you. He will serve as a mouth for you, and you will serve as God to him. ¹⁷ And take this staff in your hand that you will perform the signs with."

…

REUNION OF MOSES AND AARON

²⁷ Now the LORD had said to Aaron, "Go and meet Moses in the wilderness." So he went and met him at the mountain of God and kissed him. ²⁸ Moses told Aaron everything the LORD had sent him to say, and about all the signs he had commanded him to do. ²⁹ Then Moses and Aaron went and assembled all the elders of the Israelites. ³⁰ Aaron repeated everything the LORD had said to Moses and performed the signs before the people. ³¹ The people believed, and when they heard that the LORD had paid attention to them and that he had seen their misery, they knelt low and worshiped.

EXODUS 7:8-13

⁸ The LORD said to Moses and Aaron, ⁹ "When Pharaoh tells you, 'Perform a miracle,' tell Aaron, 'Take your staff and throw it down before Pharaoh. It will become a serpent.'" ¹⁰ So Moses and Aaron went in to Pharaoh and did just as the LORD had commanded. Aaron threw down his staff before Pharaoh and his officials, and it became a serpent. ¹¹ But then Pharaoh called the wise men and sorcerers—the magicians of Egypt, and they also did the same thing by their occult practices. ¹² Each one threw down his staff, and it became a serpent. But Aaron's staff swallowed their staffs. ¹³ However, Pharaoh's heart was hard, and he did not listen to them, as the LORD had said.

EXODUS 32:1-6, 21-24

THE GOLD CALF

¹ When the people saw that Moses delayed in coming down from the mountain, they gathered around Aaron and said to him, "Come, make gods for us who will go before

us because this Moses, the man who brought us up from the land of Egypt—we don't know what has happened to him!"

[2] Aaron replied to them, "Take off the gold rings that are on the ears of your wives, your sons, and your daughters and bring them to me." [3] So all the people took off the gold rings that were on their ears and brought them to Aaron. [4] He took the gold from them, fashioned it with an engraving tool, and made it into an image of a calf.

Then they said, "Israel, these are your gods, who brought you up from the land of Egypt!"

[5] When Aaron saw this, he built an altar in front of it and made an announcement: "There will be a festival to the LORD tomorrow." [6] Early the next morning they arose, offered burnt offerings, and presented fellowship offerings. The people sat down to eat and drink, and got up to party.

. . .

[21] Then Moses asked Aaron, "What did these people do to you that you have led them into such a grave sin?"

[22] "Don't be enraged, my lord," Aaron replied. "You yourself know that the people are intent on evil. [23] They said to me, 'Make gods for us who will go before us because this Moses, the man who brought us up from the land of Egypt—we don't know what has happened to him!' [24] So I said to them, 'Whoever has gold, take it off,' and they gave it to me. When I threw it into the fire, out came this calf!"

LEVITICUS 8:1–5

ORDINATION OF AARON AND HIS SONS

[1] The LORD spoke to Moses: [2] "Take Aaron, his sons with him, the garments, the anointing oil, the bull of the sin offering, the two rams, and the basket of unleavened bread, [3] and assemble the whole community at the entrance to the tent of meeting." [4] So Moses did as the LORD commanded him, and the community assembled at the entrance to the tent of meeting. [5] Moses said to them, "This is what the LORD has commanded to be done."

LEVITICUS 9:1-7

¹ On the eighth day Moses summoned Aaron, his sons, and the elders of Israel. ² He said to Aaron, "Take a young bull for a sin offering and a ram for a burnt offering, both without blemish, and present them before the LORD. ³ And tell the Israelites: Take a male goat for a sin offering; a calf and a lamb, male yearlings without blemish, for a burnt offering; ⁴ an ox and a ram for a fellowship offering to sacrifice before the LORD; and a grain offering mixed with oil.

FOR TODAY THE LORD IS GOING TO APPEAR TO YOU."

⁵ They brought what Moses had commanded to the front of the tent of meeting, and the whole community came forward and stood before the LORD. ⁶ Moses said, "This is what the LORD commanded you to do, that the glory of the LORD may appear to you." ⁷ Then Moses said to Aaron, "Approach the altar and sacrifice your sin offering and your burnt offering; make atonement for yourself and the people. Sacrifice the people's offering and make atonement for them, as the LORD commanded."

LEVITICUS 10:8-11

REGULATIONS FOR PRIESTS

⁸ The LORD spoke to Aaron: ⁹ "You and your sons are not to drink wine or beer when you enter the tent of meeting, or else you will die; this is a permanent statute throughout your generations. ¹⁰ You must distinguish between the holy and the common, and the clean and the unclean, ¹¹ and teach the Israelites all the statutes that the LORD has given to them through Moses."

RESPOND

1. WHERE DO I SEE GOD AT WORK IN AARON'S STORY?

2. HOW DO I CONNECT TO AARON'S EXPERIENCES? IN WHAT WAYS DO HIS EXPERIENCES FEEL FOREIGN TO ME?

3. AFTER READING AARON'S STORY, WHAT DO I WANT TO CONTINUE TO MEDITATE ON?

BEZALEL

AN ARTISAN FILLED WITH GOD'S SPIRIT

EXODUS 31:1-11

GOD'S PROVISION OF THE SKILLED WORKERS

[1] The LORD also spoke to Moses: [2] "Look, I have appointed by name Bezalel son of Uri, son of Hur, of the tribe of Judah. [3] I have filled him with God's Spirit, with wisdom, understanding, and ability in every craft [4] to design artistic works in gold, silver, and bronze, [5] to cut gemstones for mounting, and to carve wood for work in every craft. [6] I have also selected Oholiab son of Ahisamach, of the tribe of Dan, to be with him. I have put wisdom in the heart of every skilled artisan in order to make all that I have commanded you: [7] the tent of meeting, the ark of the testimony, the mercy seat that is on top of it, and all the other furnishings of the tent— [8] the table with its utensils, the pure gold lampstand with all its utensils, the altar of incense, [9] the altar of burnt offering with all its utensils, the basin with its stand— [10] the specially woven garments, both the holy garments for the priest Aaron and the garments for his sons to serve as priests, [11] the anointing oil, and the fragrant incense for the sanctuary. They must make them according to all that I have commanded you."

EXODUS 35:30-35

BEZALEL AND OHOLIAB

[30] Moses then said to the Israelites, "Look, the LORD has appointed by name Bezalel son of Uri, son of Hur, of the tribe of Judah. [31] He has filled him with God's Spirit, with wisdom, understanding, and ability in every kind of craft [32] to design artistic works in gold, silver, and bronze, [33] to cut gemstones for mounting, and to carve wood for work in every

kind of artistic craft. [34] He has also given both him and Oholiab son of Ahisamach, of the tribe of Dan, the ability to teach others. [35] He has filled them with skill to do all the work of a gem cutter; a designer; an embroiderer in blue, purple, and scarlet yarn and fine linen; and a weaver. They can do every kind of craft and design artistic designs."

EXODUS 36:1-7

[1] "Bezalel, Oholiab, and all the skilled people are to work based on everything the LORD has commanded. The LORD has given them wisdom and understanding to know how to do all the work of constructing the sanctuary."

[2] So Moses summoned Bezalel, Oholiab, and every skilled person in whose heart the LORD had placed wisdom, all whose hearts moved them, to come to the work and do it. [3] They took from Moses's presence all the contributions that the Israelites had brought for the task of making the sanctuary. Meanwhile, the people continued to bring freewill offerings morning after morning.

[4] Then all the artisans who were doing all the work for the sanctuary came one by one from the work they were doing [5] and said to Moses, "The people are bringing more than is needed for the construction of the work the LORD commanded to be done."

[6] After Moses gave an order, they sent a proclamation throughout the camp: "Let no man or woman make anything else as an offering for the sanctuary." So the people stopped. [7] The materials were sufficient for them to do all the work.

THERE WAS MORE THAN ENOUGH.

RESPOND

DATE   /   /

1. WHERE DO I SEE GOD AT WORK IN BEZALEL'S STORY?

2. HOW DO I CONNECT TO BEZALEL'S EXPERIENCES? IN WHAT WAYS DO HIS EXPERIENCES FEEL FOREIGN TO ME?

3. AFTER READING BEZALEL'S STORY, WHAT DO I WANT TO CONTINUE TO MEDITATE ON?

JOSHUA

DAY 17  WEEK 3

NUMBERS 13:1–3

SCOUTING OUT CANAAN

¹ The LORD spoke to Moses: ² "Send men to scout out the land of Canaan I am giving to the Israelites. Send one man who is a leader among them from each of their ancestral tribes." ³ Moses sent them from the Wilderness of Paran at the LORD's command. All the men were leaders in Israel.

NUMBERS 14:5–10, 26–38

⁵ Then Moses and Aaron fell facedown in front of the whole assembly of the Israelite community. ⁶ Joshua son of Nun and Caleb son of Jephunneh, who were among those who scouted out the land, tore their clothes ⁷ and said to the entire Israelite community, "The land we passed through and explored is an extremely good land. ⁸ If the LORD is pleased with us, he will bring us into this land, a land flowing with milk and honey, and give it to us. ⁹ Only don't rebel against the LORD, and don't be afraid of the people of the land, for we will devour them. Their protection has been removed from them, and the LORD is with us. Don't be afraid of them!"

¹⁰ While the whole community threatened to stone them, the glory of the LORD appeared to all the Israelites at the tent of meeting.

…

²⁶ Then the LORD spoke to Moses and Aaron: ²⁷ "How long must I endure this evil community that keeps complaining about me? I have heard the Israelites' complaints that they make against me. ²⁸ Tell them: As I live—this is the LORD's declaration—I will do to you exactly as I heard you say. ²⁹ Your corpses will fall in this wilderness—all of you who were registered in the census, the entire number of you twenty years old or more—because you have complained about me. ³⁰ I swear that none of you will enter the land I promised to settle you in, except Caleb son of Jephunneh and Joshua son of Nun. ³¹ I will bring your children whom you said would become plunder into the land you rejected, and they will enjoy it. ³² But as for you, your corpses will fall in this wilderness. ³³ Your children will be shepherds in the wilderness for forty years and bear the penalty for your acts of unfaithfulness until

all your corpses lie scattered in the wilderness. ³⁴ You will bear the consequences of your iniquities forty years based on the number of the forty days that you scouted the land, a year for each day. You will know my displeasure. ³⁵ I, the LORD, have spoken. I swear that I will do this to the entire evil community that has conspired against me. They will come to an end in the wilderness, and there they will die."

³⁶ So the men Moses sent to scout out the land, and who returned and incited the entire community to complain about him by spreading a negative report about the land— ³⁷ those men who spread the negative report about the land were struck down by the LORD. ³⁸ Only Joshua son of Nun and Caleb son of Jephunneh remained alive of those men who went to scout out the land.

JOSHUA 1:1-9

ENCOURAGEMENT OF JOSHUA

¹ After the death of Moses the LORD's servant, the LORD spoke to Joshua son of Nun, Moses's assistant: ² "Moses my servant is dead. Now you and all the people prepare to cross over the Jordan to the land I am giving the Israelites. ³ I have given you every place where the sole of your foot treads, just as I promised Moses. ⁴ Your territory will be from the wilderness and Lebanon to the great river, the Euphrates River—all the land of the Hittites—and west to the Mediterranean Sea. ⁵ No one will be able to stand against you as long as you live.

I WILL BE WITH YOU, JUST AS I WAS WITH MOSES. I WILL NOT LEAVE YOU OR ABANDON YOU.

⁶ "Be strong and courageous, for you will distribute the land I swore to their ancestors to give them as an inheritance. ⁷ Above all, be strong and very courageous to observe carefully the whole instruction my servant Moses commanded you. Do not turn from it to the right or the left, so that you will have success wherever you go. ⁸ This book of instruction must not depart from your mouth; you are to meditate on it day and night so that you may carefully observe everything written in it. For then you will prosper and succeed in whatever you do. ⁹ Haven't I commanded you: be strong and courageous? Do not be afraid or discouraged, for the LORD your God is with you wherever you go."

JOSHUA'S FAREWELL ADDRESS

¹ A long time after the LORD had given Israel rest from all the enemies around them, Joshua was old, advanced in age. ² So Joshua summoned all Israel, including its elders, leaders, judges, and officers, and said to them, "I am old, advanced in age, ³ and you have seen for yourselves everything the LORD your God did to all these nations on your account, because it was the LORD your God who was fighting for you. ⁴ See, I have allotted these remaining nations to you as an inheritance for your tribes, including all the nations I have destroyed, from the Jordan westward to the Mediterranean Sea. ⁵ The LORD your God will force them back on your account and drive them out before you so that you can take possession of their land, as the LORD your God promised you.

⁶ "Be very strong and continue obeying all that is written in the book of the law of Moses, so that you do not turn from it to the right or left ⁷ and so that you do not associate with these nations remaining among you. Do not call on the names of their gods or make an oath to them; do not serve them or bow in worship to them. ⁸ Instead, be loyal to the LORD your God, as you have been to this day.

⁹ "The LORD has driven out great and powerful nations before you, and no one is able to stand against you to this day. ¹⁰ One of you routed a thousand because the LORD your God was fighting for you, as he promised. ¹¹ So diligently watch yourselves! Love the LORD your God! ¹² If you ever turn away and become loyal to the rest of these nations remaining among you, and if you intermarry or associate with them and they with you, ¹³ know for certain that the LORD your God will not continue to drive these nations out before you. They will become a snare and a trap for you, a sharp stick for your sides and thorns in your eyes, until you disappear from this good land the LORD your God has given you.

¹⁴ "I am now going the way of the whole earth, and you know with all your heart and all your soul that none of the good promises the LORD your God made to you has failed. Everything was fulfilled for you; not one promise has failed. ¹⁵ Since every good thing the LORD your God promised you has come about, so he will bring on you every bad thing until he has annihilated you from this good land the LORD your God has given you. ¹⁶ If you break the covenant of the LORD your God, which he commanded you, and go and serve other gods, and bow in worship to them, the LORD's anger will burn against you, and you will quickly disappear from this good land he has given you."

RESPOND

1. WHERE DO I SEE GOD AT WORK IN JOSHUA'S STORY?

2. HOW DO I CONNECT TO JOSHUA'S EXPERIENCES? IN WHAT WAYS DO HIS EXPERIENCES FEEL FOREIGN TO ME?

3. AFTER READING JOSHUA'S STORY, WHAT DO I WANT TO CONTINUE TO MEDITATE ON?

RAHAB

A CANAANITE WOMAN WHO GAVE

AND RECEIVED PROTECTION

SPIES SENT TO JERICHO

[1] Joshua son of Nun secretly sent two men as spies from the Acacia Grove, saying, "Go and scout the land, especially Jericho." So they left, and they came to the house of a prostitute named Rahab, and stayed there.

[2] The king of Jericho was told, "Look, some of the Israelite men have come here tonight to investigate the land." [3] Then the king of Jericho sent word to Rahab and said, "Bring out the men who came to you and entered your house, for they came to investigate the entire land."

[4] But the woman had taken the two men and hidden them. So she said, "Yes, the men did come to me, but I didn't know where they were from. [5] At nightfall, when the city gate was about to close, the men went out, and I don't know where they were going. Chase after them quickly, and you can catch up with them!" [6] But she had taken them up to the roof and hidden them among the stalks of flax that she had arranged on the roof. [7] The men pursued them along the road to the fords of the Jordan, and as soon as they left to pursue them, the city gate was shut.

THE PROMISE TO RAHAB

[8] Before the men fell asleep, she went up on the roof [9] and said to them, "I know that the LORD has given you this land and that the terror of you has fallen on us, and everyone who lives in the land is panicking because of you. [10] For we have heard how the LORD dried up the water of the Red Sea before you when you came out of Egypt, and what you did to Sihon and Og, the two Amorite kings you completely destroyed across the Jordan. [11] When we heard this, we lost heart, and everyone's courage failed because of you, for the LORD your God is God in heaven above and on earth below. [12] Now please swear to me by the LORD that you will also show kindness to my father's family, because I showed kindness to you. Give me a sure sign [13] that you will spare the lives of my father, mother, brothers, sisters, and all who belong to them, and save us from death."

[14] The men answered her, "We will give our lives for yours. If you don't report our mission, we will show kindness and faithfulness to you when the LORD gives us the land."

[15] Then she let them down by a rope through the window, since she lived in a house that was built into the wall of the city. [16] "Go to the hill

country so that the men pursuing you won't find you," she said to them. "Hide there for three days until they return; afterward, go on your way."

[17] The men said to her, "We will be free from this oath you made us swear, [18] unless, when we enter the land, you tie this scarlet cord to the window through which you let us down. Bring your father, mother, brothers, and all your father's family into your house. [19] If anyone goes out the doors of your house, his death will be his own fault, and we will be innocent. But if anyone with you in the house should be harmed, his death will be our fault. [20] And if you report our mission, we are free from the oath you made us swear."

[21] "Let it be as you say," she replied, and she sent them away. After they had gone, she tied the scarlet cord to the window.

[22] So the two men went into the hill country and stayed there three days until the pursuers had returned. They searched all along the way, but did not find them. [23] Then the men returned, came down from the hill country, and crossed the Jordan. They went to Joshua son of Nun and reported everything that had happened to them. [24] They told Joshua, "The Lord has handed over the entire land to us. Everyone who lives in the land is also panicking because of us."

JOSHUA 6:22-25

RAHAB AND HER FAMILY SPARED

[22] Joshua said to the two men who had scouted the land, "Go to the prostitute's house and bring the woman out of there, and all who are with her, just as you swore to her." [23] So the young men who had scouted went in and brought out Rahab and her father, mother, brothers, and all who belonged to her. They brought out her whole family and settled them outside the camp of Israel.

[24] They burned the city and everything in it, but they put the silver and gold and the articles of bronze and iron into the treasury of the Lord's house. [25] However, Joshua spared Rahab the prostitute, her father's family, and all who belonged to her, because she hid the messengers Joshua had sent to spy on Jericho, and she still lives in Israel today.

RESPOND

DATE   /   /

1. WHERE DO I SEE GOD AT WORK IN RAHAB'S STORY?

2. HOW DO I CONNECT TO RAHAB'S EXPERIENCES? IN WHAT WAYS DO HER EXPERIENCES FEEL FOREIGN TO ME?

3. AFTER READING RAHAB'S STORY, WHAT DO I WANT TO CONTINUE TO MEDITATE ON?

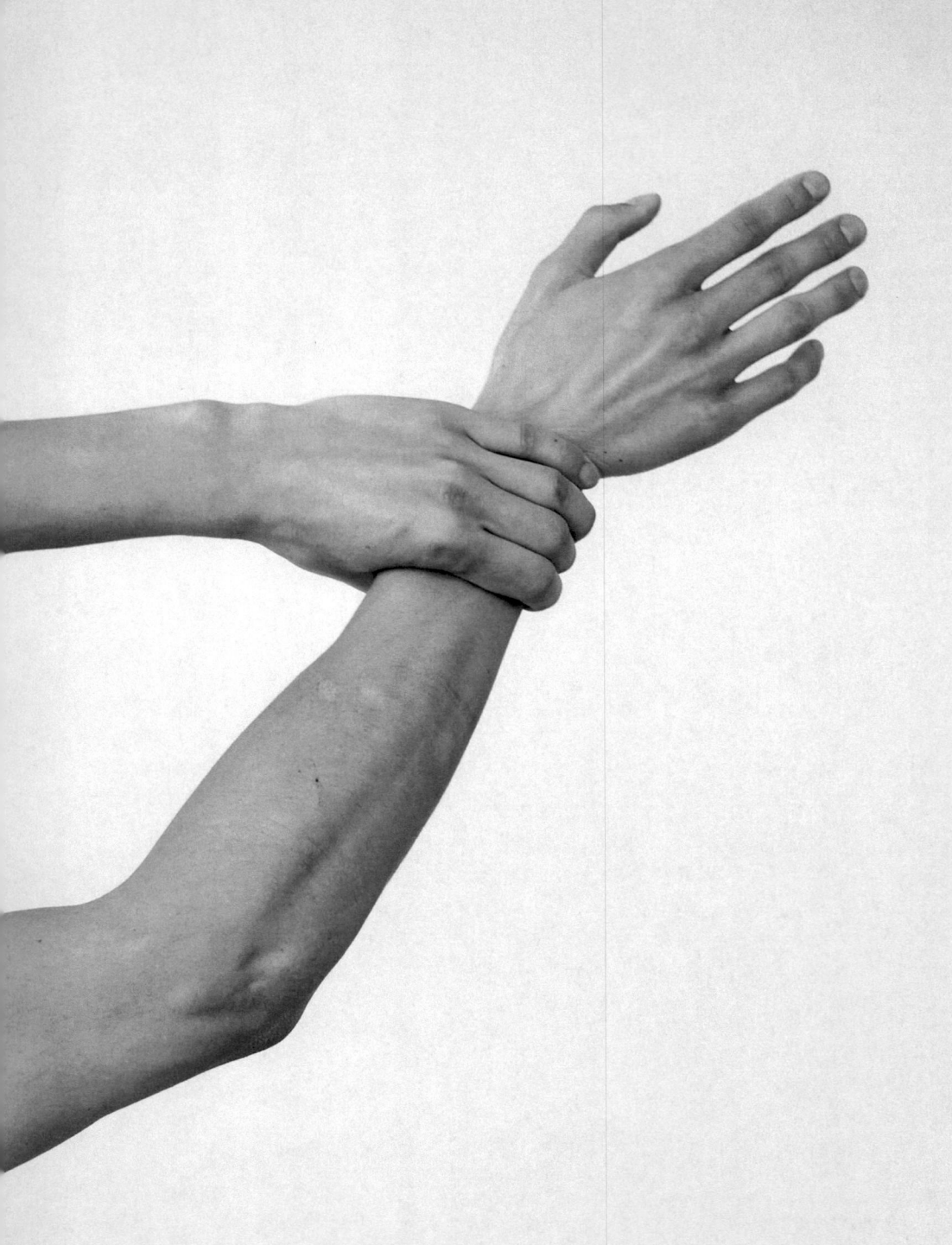

DEBORAH
A PROPHETESS AND JUDGE

JUDGES 4

DEBORAH AND BARAK

¹ The Israelites again did what was evil in the sight of the LORD after Ehud had died. ² So the LORD sold them to King Jabin of Canaan, who reigned in Hazor. The commander of his army was Sisera who lived in Harosheth of the Nations. ³ Then the Israelites cried out to the LORD, because Jabin had nine hundred iron chariots, and he harshly oppressed them twenty years.

⁴ Deborah, a prophetess and the wife of Lappidoth, was judging Israel at that time. ⁵ She would sit under the palm tree of Deborah between Ramah and Bethel in the hill country of Ephraim, and the Israelites went up to her to settle disputes.

⁶ She summoned Barak son of Abinoam from Kedesh in Naphtali and said to him, "Hasn't the LORD, the God of Israel, commanded you, 'Go, deploy the troops on Mount Tabor, and take with you ten thousand men from the Naphtalites and Zebulunites? ⁷ Then I will lure Sisera commander of Jabin's army, his chariots, and his infantry at the Wadi Kishon to fight against you, and I will hand him over to you.'"

⁸ Barak said to her, "If you will go with me, I will go. But if you will not go with me, I will not go."

⁹ "I WILL GLADLY GO WITH YOU,"

she said, "but you will receive no honor on the road you are about to take, because the LORD will sell Sisera to a woman." So Deborah got up and went with Barak to Kedesh. ¹⁰ Barak summoned Zebulun and Naphtali to Kedesh; ten thousand men followed him, and Deborah also went with him.

¹¹ Now Heber the Kenite had moved away from the Kenites, the sons of Hobab, Moses's father-in-law, and pitched his tent beside the oak tree of Zaanannim, which was near Kedesh.

¹² It was reported to Sisera that Barak son of Abinoam had gone up Mount Tabor. ¹³ Sisera summoned all his nine hundred iron chariots and all the troops who were with him from Harosheth of the Nations to the Wadi Kishon. ¹⁴ Then Deborah said to Barak, "Go! This is the day the LORD has handed Sisera over to you. Hasn't the LORD gone before you?" So Barak came down from Mount Tabor with ten thousand men following him.

¹⁵ The LORD threw Sisera, all his charioteers, and all his army into a panic before Barak's assault. Sisera left his chariot and fled on foot. ¹⁶ Barak pursued the chariots and the army as far as Harosheth of the Nations, and the whole army of Sisera fell by the sword; not a single man was left.

¹⁷ Meanwhile, Sisera had fled on foot to the tent of Jael, the wife of Heber the Kenite, because there was peace between King Jabin of Hazor and the family of Heber the Kenite. ¹⁸ Jael went out to greet Sisera and said to him, "Come in, my lord. Come in with me. Don't be afraid." So he went into her tent, and she covered him with a blanket. ¹⁹ He said to her, "Please give me a little water to drink for I am thirsty." She opened a container of milk, gave him a drink, and covered him again. ²⁰ Then he said to her, "Stand at the entrance to the tent. If a man comes and asks you, 'Is there a man here?' say, 'No.'" ²¹ While he was sleeping from exhaustion, Heber's wife, Jael, took a tent peg, grabbed a hammer, and went silently to Sisera. She hammered the peg into his temple and drove it into the ground, and he died.

²² When Barak arrived in pursuit of Sisera, Jael went out to greet him and said to him, "Come and I will show you the man you are looking for." So he went in with her, and there was Sisera lying dead with a tent peg through his temple!

²³ That day God subdued King Jabin of Canaan before the Israelites. ²⁴ The power of the Israelites continued to increase against King Jabin of Canaan until they destroyed him.

JUDGES 5

DEBORAH'S SONG

¹ On that day Deborah and Barak son of Abinoam sang:

² When the leaders lead in Israel,
when the people volunteer,
blessed be the LORD.
³ Listen, kings! Pay attention, princes!
I will sing to the LORD;
I will sing praise to the LORD God of Israel.

⁴ Lord, when you came from Seir,
when you marched from the fields of Edom,
the earth trembled,
the skies poured rain,
and the clouds poured water.
⁵ The mountains melted before the Lord,
even Sinai, before the Lord, the God of Israel.

⁶ In the days of Shamgar son of Anath,
in the days of Jael,
the main roads were deserted
because travelers kept to the side roads.
⁷ Villages were deserted,
they were deserted in Israel,
until I, Deborah, arose,
a mother in Israel.
⁸ Israel chose new gods,
then there was war in the city gates.
Not a shield or spear was seen
among forty thousand in Israel.
⁹ My heart is with the leaders of Israel,
with the volunteers of the people.
Blessed be the Lord!
¹⁰ You who ride on white donkeys,
who sit on saddle blankets,
and who travel on the road, give praise!
¹¹ Let them tell the righteous acts of the Lord,
the righteous deeds of his villagers in Israel,
with the voices of the singers at the watering places.
Then the Lord's people went down to the city gates.
¹² "Awake! Awake, Deborah!
Awake! Awake, sing a song!
Arise, Barak,
and take your prisoners,
son of Abinoam!"
¹³ Then the survivors came down to the nobles;
the Lord's people came down to me against the warriors.
¹⁴ Those with their roots in Amalek came from Ephraim;
Benjamin came with your people after you.
The leaders came down from Machir,
and those who carry a marshal's staff came from Zebulun.

¹⁵ The princes of Issachar were with Deborah;
Issachar was with Barak;
they were under his leadership in the valley.
There was great searching of heart
among the clans of Reuben.
¹⁶ Why did you sit among the sheep pens
listening to the playing of pipes for
   the flocks?
There was great searching of heart
among the clans of Reuben.
¹⁷ Gilead remained beyond the Jordan.
Dan, why did you linger at the ships?
Asher remained at the seashore
and stayed in his harbors.
¹⁸ The people of Zebulun defied death,
Naphtali also, on the heights of
   the battlefield.

¹⁹ Kings came and fought.
Then the kings of Canaan fought
at Taanach by the Waters of Megiddo,
but they did not plunder the silver.
²⁰ The stars fought from the heavens;
the stars fought with Sisera from their paths.
²¹ The river Kishon swept them away,
the ancient river, the river Kishon.
March on, my soul, in strength!
²² The horses' hooves then hammered—
the galloping, galloping of his stallions.
²³ "Curse Meroz," says the angel of the LORD,
"Bitterly curse her inhabitants,
for they did not come to help the LORD,
to help the LORD with the warriors."

²⁴ Most blessed of women is Jael,
the wife of Heber the Kenite;

she is most blessed among
   tent-dwelling women.
²⁵ He asked for water; she gave him milk.
She brought him cream in a
   majestic bowl.
²⁶ She reached for a tent peg,
her right hand, for a workman's hammer.
Then she hammered Sisera—
she crushed his head;
she shattered and pierced his temple.
²⁷ He collapsed, he fell, he lay down between
   her feet;
he collapsed, he fell between her feet;
where he collapsed, there he fell—dead.

²⁸ Sisera's mother looked through
   the window;
she peered through the lattice, crying out:
"Why is his chariot so long in coming?
Why don't I hear the hoofbeats of
   his horses?"
²⁹ Her wisest princesses answer her;
she even answers herself:
³⁰ "Are they not finding and dividing
   the spoil—
a girl or two for each warrior,
the spoil of colored garments for Sisera,
the spoil of an embroidered garment or two
   for my neck?"

³¹ LORD, may all your enemies perish as
   Sisera did.
But may those who love him
be like the rising of the sun in its strength.

And the land had peace for forty years.

RESPOND

1. WHERE DO I SEE GOD AT WORK IN DEBORAH'S STORY?

2. HOW DO I CONNECT TO DEBORAH'S EXPERIENCES? IN WHAT WAYS DO HER EXPERIENCES FEEL FOREIGN TO ME?

3. AFTER READING DEBORAH'S STORY, WHAT DO I WANT TO CONTINUE TO MEDITATE ON?

GRACE DAY

TAKE THIS DAY TO CATCH UP ON
YOUR READING, PRAY, AND REST IN
THE PRESENCE OF THE LORD.

FOR I AM PERSUADED THAT NEITHER
DEATH NOR LIFE, NOR ANGELS NOR
RULERS, NOR THINGS PRESENT NOR
THINGS TO COME, NOR POWERS, NOR
HEIGHT NOR DEPTH, NOR ANY OTHER
CREATED THING WILL BE ABLE TO
SEPARATE US FROM THE LOVE OF GOD
THAT IS IN CHRIST JESUS OUR LORD.

ROMANS 8:38–39

WEEKLY

DAY

SCRIPTURE IS GOD BREATHED AND TRUE. WHEN WE MEMORIZE IT, WE CARRY THE GOOD NEWS OF JESUS WITH US WHEREVER WE GO.

FOR THIS PLAN, WE ARE MEMORIZING OUR KEY PASSAGE, PSALM 8:3–4. WE WILL CONTINUE WITH THE THIRD LINE.

SEE TIPS FOR MEMORIZING SCRIPTURE ON PAGE 236.

TRUTH

PSALM 8:3–4

WHEN I OBSERVE YOUR HEAVENS,
THE WORK OF YOUR FINGERS,
THE MOON AND THE STARS,
WHICH YOU SET IN PLACE,
WHAT IS A HUMAN BEING THAT YOU REMEMBER HIM,
A SON OF MAN THAT YOU LOOK AFTER HIM?

SAMSON

THE JUDGE WHO WAS DECEIVED

HE CALLED OUT TO THE LORD, "LORD GOD,
PLEASE REMEMBER ME. STRENGTHEN ME, GOD,
JUST ONCE MORE. —JUDGES 16:28

DAY 22   WEEK 4

BIRTH OF SAMSON

[1] The Israelites again did what was evil in the LORD's sight, so the LORD handed them over to the Philistines forty years. [2] There was a certain man from Zorah, from the family of Dan, whose name was Manoah; his wife was unable to conceive and had no children. [3] The angel of the LORD appeared to the woman and said to her, "Although you are unable to conceive and have no children, you will conceive and give birth to a son. [4] Now please be careful not to drink wine or beer, or to eat anything unclean; [5] for indeed, you will conceive and give birth to a son. You must never cut his hair, because the boy will be a Nazirite to God from birth, and he will begin to save Israel from the power of the Philistines."

[6] Then the woman went and told her husband, "A man of God came to me. He looked like the awe-inspiring angel of God. I didn't ask him where he came from, and he didn't tell me his name. [7] He said to me, 'You will conceive and give birth to a son. Therefore, do not drink wine or beer, and do not eat anything unclean, because the boy will be a Nazirite to God from birth until the day of his death.'"

[8] Manoah prayed to the LORD and said, "Please, Lord, let the man of God you sent come again to us and teach us what we should do for the boy who will be born."

[9] God listened to Manoah, and the angel of God came again to the woman. She was sitting in the field, and her husband, Manoah, was not with her. [10] The woman ran quickly to her husband and told him, "The man who came to me the other day has just come back!"

[11] So Manoah got up and followed his wife. When he came to the man, he asked, "Are you the man who spoke to my wife?"

"I am," he said.

[12] Then Manoah asked, "When your words come true, what will be the boy's responsibilities and work?"

[13] The angel of the LORD answered Manoah, "Your wife needs to do everything I told her. [14] She must not eat anything that comes from the

grapevine or drink wine or beer. And she must not eat anything unclean. Your wife must do everything I have commanded her."

...

24 So the woman gave birth to a son and named him Samson. The boy grew, and the LORD blessed him. 25 Then the Spirit of the LORD began to stir him in the Camp of Dan, between Zorah and Eshtaol.

JUDGES 16

SAMSON AND DELILAH

1 Samson went to Gaza, where he saw a prostitute and went to bed with her. 2 When the Gazites heard that Samson was there, they surrounded the place and waited in ambush for him all that night at the city gate. They kept quiet all night, saying, "Let's wait until dawn; then we will kill him." 3 But Samson stayed in bed only until midnight. Then he got up, took hold of the doors of the city gate along with the two gateposts, and pulled them out, bar and all. He put them on his shoulders and took them to the top of the mountain overlooking Hebron.

4 Some time later, he fell in love with a woman named Delilah, who lived in the Sorek Valley. 5 The Philistine leaders went to her and said, "Persuade him to tell you where his great strength comes from, so we can overpower him, tie him up, and make him helpless. Each of us will then give you 1,100 pieces of silver."

6 So Delilah said to Samson, "Please tell me, where does your great strength come from? How could someone tie you up and make you helpless?"

7 Samson told her, "If they tie me up with seven fresh bowstrings that have not been dried, I will become weak and be like any other man."

8 The Philistine leaders brought her seven fresh bowstrings that had not been dried, and she tied him up with them. 9 While the men in ambush were waiting in her room, she called out to him, "Samson, the Philistines are here!" But he snapped the bowstrings as a strand of yarn snaps when it touches fire. The secret of his strength remained unknown.

10 Then Delilah said to Samson, "You have mocked me and told me lies! Won't you please tell me how you can be tied up?"

[11] He told her, "If they tie me up with new ropes that have never been used, I will become weak and be like any other man."

[12] Delilah took new ropes, tied him up with them, and shouted, "Samson, the Philistines are here!" But while the men in ambush were waiting in her room, he snapped the ropes off his arms like a thread.

[13] Then Delilah said to Samson, "You have mocked me all along and told me lies! Tell me how you can be tied up."

He told her, "If you weave the seven braids on my head into the fabric on a loom—"

[14] She fastened the braids with a pin and called to him, "Samson, the Philistines are here!" He awoke from his sleep and pulled out the pin, with the loom and the web.

[15] "How can you say, 'I love you,'" she told him, "when your heart is not with me? This is the third time you have mocked me and not told me what makes your strength so great!"

[16] Because she nagged him day after day and pleaded with him until she wore him out, [17] he told her the whole truth and said to her, "My hair has never been cut, because I am a Nazirite to God from birth. If I am shaved, my strength will leave me, and I will become weak and be like any other man."

[18] When Delilah realized that he had told her the whole truth, she sent this message to the Philistine leaders: "Come one more time, for he has told me the whole truth." The Philistine leaders came to her and brought the silver with them.

[19] Then she let him fall asleep on her lap and called a man to shave off the seven braids on his head. In this way, she made him helpless, and his strength left him. [20] Then she cried, "Samson, the Philistines are here!" When he awoke from his sleep, he said, "I will escape as I did before and shake myself free."

BUT HE DID NOT KNOW THAT THE LORD
HAD LEFT HIM.

[21] The Philistines seized him and gouged out his eyes. They brought him down to Gaza and bound him with bronze shackles, and he was forced to grind grain in the prison. [22] But his hair began to grow back after it had been shaved.

[23] Now the Philistine leaders gathered together to offer a great sacrifice to their god Dagon. They rejoiced and said:

> Our god has handed over
> our enemy Samson to us.

[24] When the people saw him, they praised their god and said:

> Our god has handed over to us
> our enemy who destroyed our land
> and who multiplied our dead.

[25] When they were in good spirits, they said, "Bring Samson here to entertain us." So they brought Samson from prison, and he entertained them. They had him stand between the pillars.

[26] Samson said to the young man who was leading him by the hand, "Lead me where I can feel the pillars supporting the temple, so I can lean against them." [27] The temple was full of men and women; all the leaders of the Philistines were there, and about three thousand men and women were on the roof watching Samson entertain them. [28] He called out to the LORD, "Lord GOD, please remember me. Strengthen me, God, just once more. With one act of vengeance, let me pay back the Philistines for my two eyes." [29] Samson took hold of the two middle pillars supporting the temple and leaned against them, one on his right hand and the other on his left. [30] Samson said, "Let me die with the Philistines." He pushed with all his might, and the temple fell on the leaders and all the people in it. And those he killed at his death were more than those he had killed in his life.

[31] Then his brothers and his father's whole family came down, carried him back, and buried him between Zorah and Eshtaol in the tomb of his father Manoah. So he judged Israel twenty years.

RESPOND

01 WHERE DO I SEE GOD AT WORK IN SAMSON'S STORY?

_____
_____
_____
_____
_____
_____
_____
_____
_____
_____
_____

02 HOW DO I CONNECT TO SAMSON'S EXPERIENCES? IN WHAT WAYS DO HIS EXPERIENCES FEEL FOREIGN TO ME?

_____
_____
_____
_____
_____
_____
_____
_____
_____
_____
_____

03 AFTER READING SAMSON'S STORY, WHAT DO I WANT TO CONTINUE TO MEDITATE ON?

_____
_____
_____
_____
_____
_____
_____
_____
_____

NAOMI & RUTH

RUTH 1

NAOMI'S FAMILY IN MOAB

¹ During the time of the judges, there was a famine in the land. A man left Bethlehem in Judah with his wife and two sons to stay in the territory of Moab for a while. ² The man's name was Elimelech, and his wife's name was Naomi. The names of his two sons were Mahlon and Chilion. They were Ephrathites from Bethlehem in Judah. They entered the fields of Moab and settled there. ³ Naomi's husband, Elimelech, died, and she was left with her two sons. ⁴ Her sons took Moabite women as their wives: one was named Orpah and the second was named Ruth. After they lived in Moab about ten years, ⁵ both Mahlon and Chilion also died, and the woman was left without her two children and without her husband.

RUTH'S LOYALTY TO NAOMI

⁶ She and her daughters-in-law set out to return from the territory of Moab, because she had heard in Moab that the Lord had paid attention to his people's need by providing them food. ⁷ She left the place where she had been living, accompanied by her two daughters-in-law, and traveled along the road leading back to the land of Judah.

⁸ Naomi said to them, "Each of you go back to your mother's home. May the Lord show kindness to you as you have shown to the dead and to me. ⁹ May the Lord grant each of you rest in the house of a new husband." She kissed them, and they wept loudly.

¹⁰ They said to her, "We insist on returning with you to your people."

¹¹ But Naomi replied, "Return home, my daughters. Why do you want to go with me? Am I able to have any more sons who could become your husbands? ¹² Return home, my daughters. Go on, for I am too old to have another husband. Even if I thought there was still hope for me to have a husband tonight and to bear sons, ¹³ would you be willing to wait for them to grow up? Would you restrain yourselves from remarrying? No, my daughters, my life is much too bitter for you to share,

because the Lord's hand has turned against me." ¹⁴ Again they wept loudly, and Orpah kissed her mother-in-law, but Ruth clung to her. ¹⁵ Naomi said, "Look, your sister-in-law has gone back to her people and to her gods. Follow your sister-in-law."

¹⁶ But Ruth replied:

> Don't plead with me to abandon you
> or to return and not follow you.
> For wherever you go, I will go,
> and wherever you live, I will live;
> your people will be my people,
> and your God will be my God.
> ¹⁷ Where you die, I will die,
> and there I will be buried.
> May the Lord punish me,
> and do so severely,
> if anything but death separates you and me.

¹⁸ When Naomi saw that Ruth was determined to go with her, she stopped talking to her.

¹⁹ The two of them traveled until they came to Bethlehem. When they entered Bethlehem, the whole town was excited about their arrival and the local women exclaimed, "Can this be Naomi?"

²⁰ "Don't call me Naomi. Call me Mara," she answered, "for the Almighty has made me very bitter. ²¹ I went away full, but the Lord has brought me back empty. Why do you call me Naomi, since the Lord has opposed me, and the Almighty has afflicted me?"

²² So Naomi came back from the territory of Moab with her daughter-in-law Ruth the Moabitess. They arrived in Bethlehem at the beginning of the barley harvest.

RUTH 2:1-13, 18-20

RUTH AND BOAZ MEET

¹ Now Naomi had a relative on her husband's side. He was a prominent man of noble character from Elimelech's family. His name was Boaz.

[2] Ruth the Moabitess asked Naomi, "Will you let me go into the fields and gather fallen grain behind someone with whom I find favor?"

Naomi answered her, "Go ahead, my daughter." [3] So Ruth left and entered the field to gather grain behind the harvesters. She happened to be in the portion of the field belonging to Boaz, who was from Elimelech's family.

[4] Later, when Boaz arrived from Bethlehem, he said to the harvesters, "The LORD be with you."

"The LORD bless you," they replied.

[5] Boaz asked his servant who was in charge of the harvesters, "Whose young woman is this?"

[6] The servant answered, "She is the young Moabite woman who returned with Naomi from the territory of Moab. [7] She asked, 'Will you let me gather fallen grain among the bundles behind the harvesters?' She came and has been on her feet since early morning, except that she rested a little in the shelter."

[8] Then Boaz said to Ruth, "Listen, my daughter. Don't go and gather grain in another field, and don't leave this one, but stay here close to my female servants. [9] See which field they are harvesting, and follow them. Haven't I ordered the young men not to touch you? When you are thirsty, go and drink from the jars the young men have filled."

[10] She fell facedown, bowed to the ground, and said to him, "Why have I found favor with you, so that you notice me, although I am a foreigner?"

[11] Boaz answered her, "Everything you have done for your mother-in-law since your husband's death has been fully reported to me: how you left your father and mother and your native land, and how you came to a people you didn't previously know. [12] May the LORD reward you for what you have done, and may you receive a full reward from the LORD God of Israel, under whose wings you have come for refuge."

[13] "My lord," she said, "I have found favor with you, for you have comforted and encouraged your servant, although I am not like one of your female servants."

. . .

[18] She picked up the grain and went into the town, where her mother-in-law saw what she had gleaned. She brought out what she had left over from her meal and gave it to her.

[19] Her mother-in-law said to her, "Where did you gather barley today, and where did you work? May the LORD bless the man who noticed you."

Ruth told her mother-in-law whom she had worked with and said, "The name of the man I worked with today is Boaz."

[20] Then Naomi said to her daughter-in-law, "May the LORD bless him because he has not abandoned his kindness to the living or the dead." Naomi continued, "The man is a close relative. He is one of our family redeemers."

RUTH 3:1-11

RUTH'S APPEAL TO BOAZ

[1] Ruth's mother-in-law Naomi said to her, "My daughter, shouldn't I find rest for you, so that you will be taken care of? [2] Now isn't Boaz our relative? Haven't you been working with his female servants? This evening he will be

winnowing barley on the threshing floor. ³ Wash, put on perfumed oil, and wear your best clothes. Go down to the threshing floor, but don't let the man know you are there until he has finished eating and drinking. ⁴ When he lies down, notice the place where he's lying, go in and uncover his feet, and lie down. Then he will explain to you what you should do."

⁵ So Ruth said to her, "I will do everything you say." ⁶ She went down to the threshing floor and did everything her mother-in-law had charged her to do. ⁷ After Boaz ate, drank, and was in good spirits, he went to lie down at the end of the pile of barley, and she came secretly, uncovered his feet, and lay down.

⁸ At midnight, Boaz was startled, turned over, and there lying at his feet was a woman! ⁹ So he asked, "Who are you?"

"I am Ruth, your servant," she replied. "Take me under your wing, for you are a family redeemer."

¹⁰ Then he said, "May the LORD bless you, my daughter. You have shown more kindness now than before, because you have not pursued younger men, whether rich or poor. ¹¹ Now don't be afraid, my daughter. I will do for you whatever you say, since all the people in my town know that you are a woman of noble character."

RUTH 4:1–6, 13–17

RUTH AND BOAZ MARRY

¹ Boaz went to the gate of the town and sat down there. Soon the family redeemer Boaz had spoken about came by. Boaz said, "Come over here and sit down." So he went over and sat down. ² Then Boaz took ten men of the town's elders and said, "Sit here." And they sat down. ³ He said to the redeemer, "Naomi, who has returned from the territory of Moab, is selling the portion of the field that belonged to our brother Elimelech. ⁴ I thought I should inform you: Buy it back in the presence of those seated here and in the presence of the elders of my people. If you want to redeem it, do it. But if you do not want to redeem it, tell me so that I will know, because there isn't anyone other than you to redeem it, and I am next after you."

"I want to redeem it," he answered.

⁵ Then Boaz said, "On the day you buy the field from Naomi, you will acquire Ruth the Moabitess, the wife of the deceased man, to perpetuate the man's name on his property."

⁶ The redeemer replied, "I can't redeem it myself, or I will ruin my own inheritance. Take my right of redemption, because I can't redeem it."

. . .

¹³ Boaz took Ruth and she became his wife. He slept with her, and the LORD granted conception to her, and she gave birth to a son. ¹⁴ The women said to Naomi,

"BLESSED BE THE LORD, WHO HAS NOT LEFT YOU WITHOUT A FAMILY REDEEMER TODAY. MAY HIS NAME BECOME WELL KNOWN IN ISRAEL.

¹⁵ He will renew your life and sustain you in your old age. Indeed, your daughter-in-law, who loves you and is better to you than seven sons, has given birth to him." ¹⁶ Naomi took the child, placed him on her lap, and became a mother to him. ¹⁷ The neighbor women said, "A son has been born to Naomi," and they named him Obed. He was the father of Jesse, the father of David.

RESPOND

01 WHERE DO I SEE GOD AT WORK IN
    NAOMI AND RUTH'S STORY?

_____

_____

_____

_____

_____

_____

_____

_____

_____

_____

02 HOW DO I CONNECT TO NAOMI AND
    RUTH'S EXPERIENCES? IN WHAT
    WAYS DO THEIR EXPERIENCES FEEL
    FOREIGN TO ME?

_____

_____

_____

_____

_____

_____

_____

_____

_____

03 AFTER READING NAOMI AND RUTH'S STORY, WHAT DO I WANT TO CONTINUE TO
    MEDITATE ON?

_____

_____

_____

_____

_____

_____

_____

_____

CONNECTING THE STORIES

KEY

■ Creation and the Patriarchs

■ The Exodus, the Wilderness, and the Promised Land

■ The Judges

——— Indicates a passage of time

∼∼∼ Indicates an extended passage of time

○ Indicates members of Jesus's family line

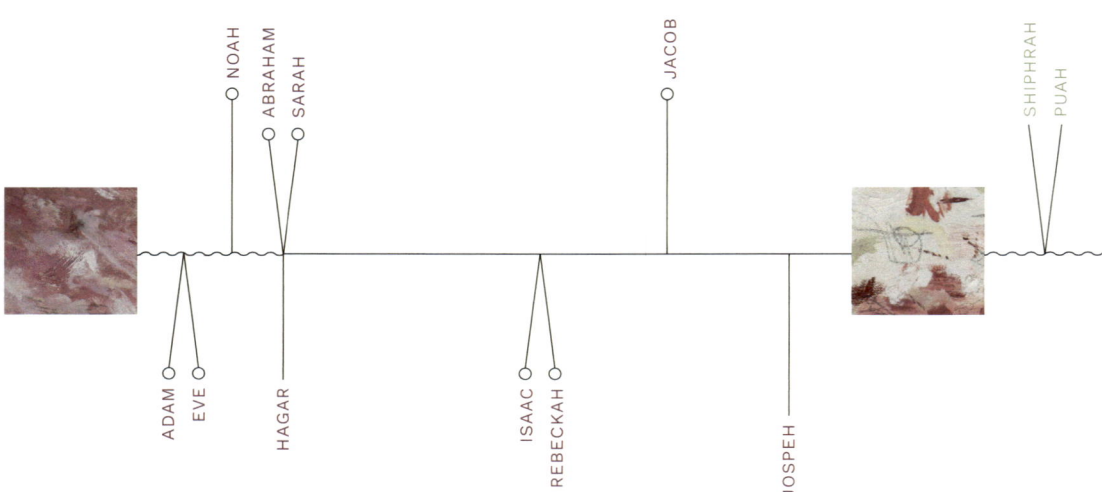

○ NOAH ○ ABRAHAM SARAH ○ JACOB SHIPHRAH PUAH

ADAM EVE HAGAR ISAAC REBECKAH JOSPEH

CREATION AND THE PATRIARCHS

ADAM and **EVE** were the first humans.

NOAH descended from one of **ADAM** and **EVE'S** sons.

ABRAHAM descended from one of **NOAH'S** sons.

ABRAHAM and **SARAH** were married.

HAGAR was **SARAH'S** Egyptian slave who was given to **ABRAHAM** to bear a son.

ISAAC was the first and only son of **ABRAHAM** and **SARAH**.

REBEKAH was married to **ISAAC** and was the granddaughter of **ABRAHAM'S** brother.

JACOB was the youngest twin of **ISAAC** and **REBEKAH**.

JOSEPH was the son of **JACOB**.

All thirty-nine books of the Old Testament combine to tell a single story—the story of God and His love for humanity. When we read these individual stories, it can be easy to miss the connections—whether in time periods or through events or family lines—that are present between these people. On the following pages, you will find a graphic representing some of the ways the people in this reading plan are connected to one another across time. Below the timeline, you will find details about the interpersonal connections among many of these stories.

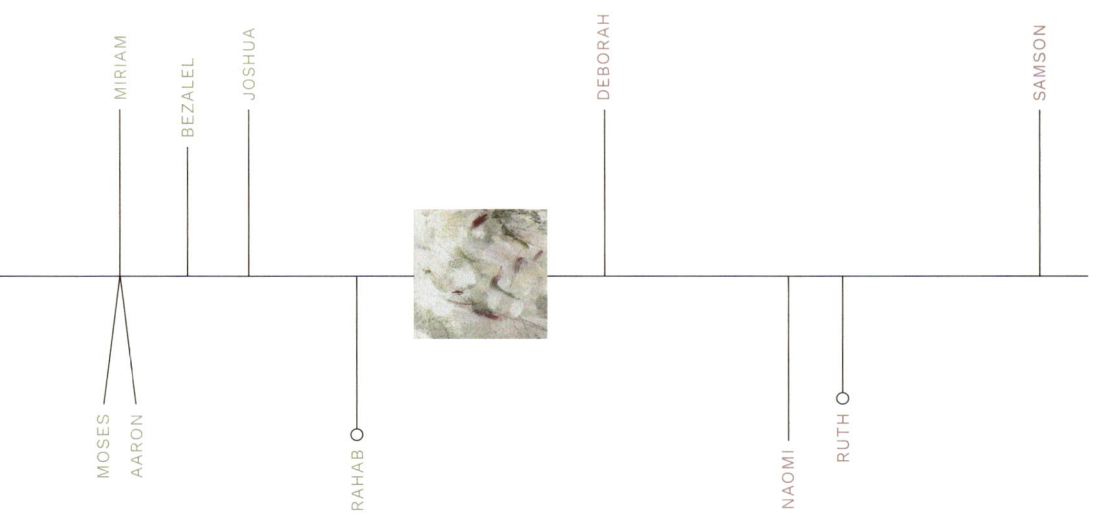

MIRIAM
BEZALEL
JOSHUA
DEBORAH
SAMSON

MOSES
AARON
RAHAB
NAOMI
RUTH

THE EXODUS, THE WILDERNESS, AND THE PROMISED LAND

MIRIAM, **AARON**, and **MOSES** were siblings.

BEZALEL was called on by **MOSES** to be the chief artisan of the tabernacle.

During the wilderness years, **JOSHUA** rose up in leadership under **MOSES'S** guidance.

RAHAB protected the spies that **JOSHUA** sent into Jericho.

THE JUDGES

NAOMI was **RUTH'S** mother-in-law.

KEY

- ■ The United Kingdom of Israel
- ■ The Divided Kingdoms of Israel and Judah
- ■ The Exile
- ■ The Exilic Return

- —— Indicates a passage of time
- ~~ Indicates an extended passage of time
- ○ Indicates members of Jesus's family line

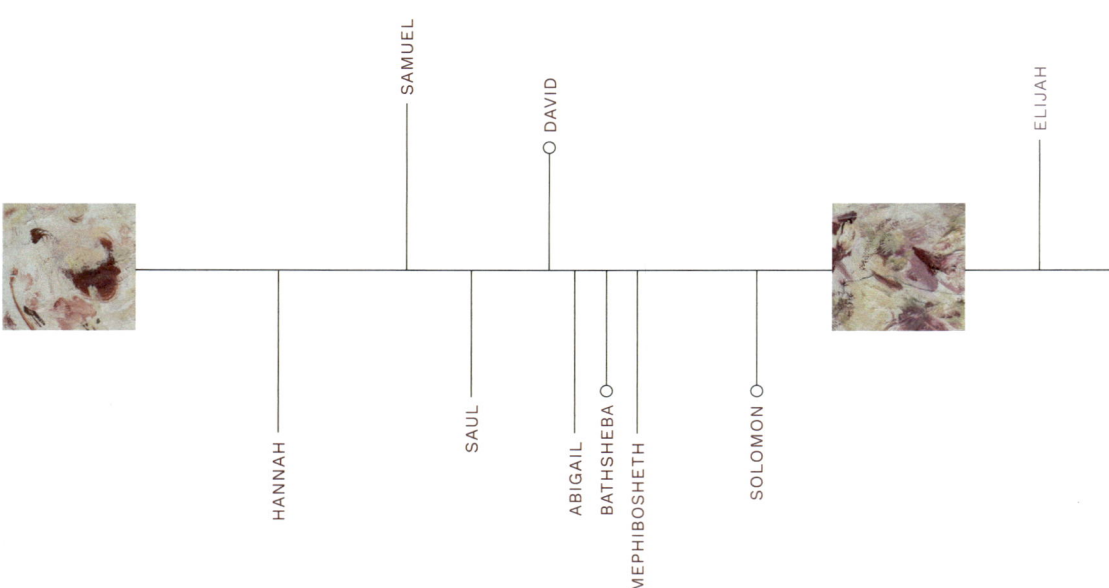

SAMUEL

○ DAVID

ELIJAH

HANNAH

SAUL

ABIGAIL

BATHSHEBA ○

MEPHIBOSHETH

SOLOMON ○

THE UNITED KINGDOM OF ISRAEL

HANNAH was the mother of **SAMUEL**.

SAMUEL anointed both **SAUL** and **DAVID** as kings.

DAVID descended from the line of **RUTH**.

ABIGAIL was one of **DAVID'S** wives.

MEPHIBOSHETH was the grandson of **SAUL**; **MEPHIBOSHETH** was invited into **DAVID'S** home after **SAUL'S** death.

BATHSHEBA was one of **DAVID'S** wives.

SOLOMON was the son of **DAVID** and **BATHSHEBA**.

THE DIVIDED KINGDOMS OF ISRAEL AND JUDAH

HOSEA and **GOMER** were married.

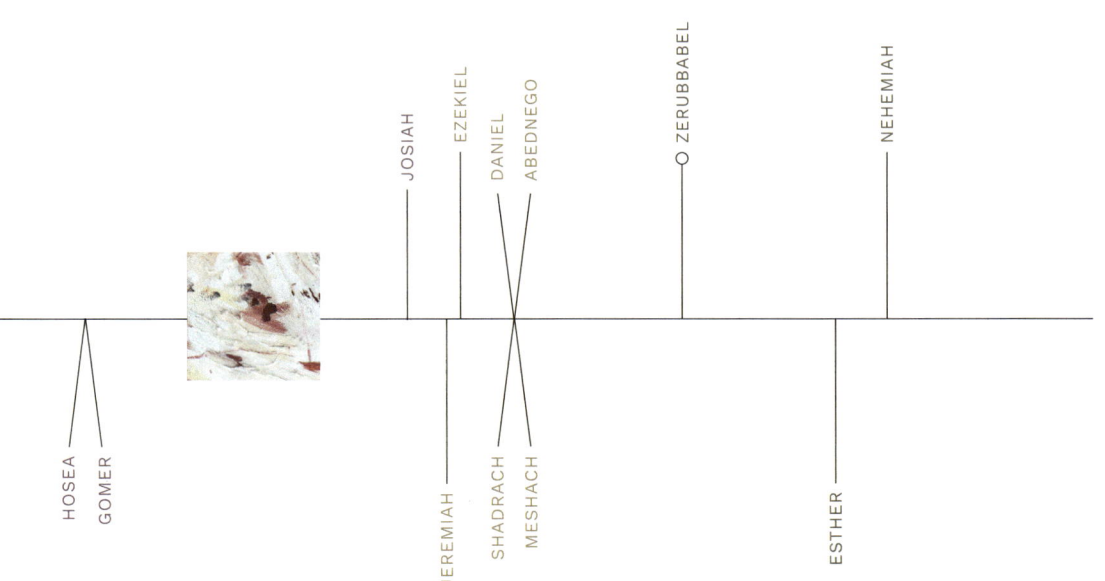

JOSIAH

EZEKIEL

DANIEL

ABEDNEGO

ZERUBBABEL

NEHEMIAH

HOSEA

GOMER

JEREMIAH

SHADRACH

MESHACH

ESTHER

THE EXILE

DANIEL, SHADRACH, MESHACH, and **ABEDNEGO** were all exiled to Babylon together.

THE EXILIC RETURN

ZERUBBABEL was tasked with rebuilding the temple in Jerusalem; **NEHEMIAH** built the walls surrounding the city to protect it.

HANNAH
THE CHILDLESS WOMAN
HEARD BY GOD

1 SAMUEL 1

HANNAH'S VOW

¹ There was a man from Ramathaim-zophim in the hill country of Ephraim. His name was Elkanah son of Jeroham, son of Elihu, son of Tohu, son of Zuph, an Ephraimite. ² He had two wives, the first named Hannah and the second Peninnah. Peninnah had children, but Hannah was childless. ³ This man would go up from his town every year to worship and to sacrifice to the LORD of Armies at Shiloh, where Eli's two sons, Hophni and Phinehas, were the LORD's priests.

⁴ Whenever Elkanah offered a sacrifice, he always gave portions of the meat to his wife Peninnah and to each of her sons and daughters. ⁵ But he gave a double portion to Hannah, for he loved her even though the LORD had kept her from conceiving. ⁶ Her rival would taunt her severely just to provoke her, because the LORD had kept Hannah from conceiving. ⁷ Year after year, when she went up to the LORD's house, her rival taunted her in this way. Hannah would weep and would not eat. ⁸ "Hannah, why are you crying?" her husband, Elkanah, would ask. "Why won't you eat? Why are you troubled? Am I not better to you than ten sons?"

⁹ On one occasion, Hannah got up after they ate and drank at Shiloh. The priest Eli was sitting on a chair by the doorpost of the LORD's temple. ¹⁰ Deeply hurt, Hannah prayed to the LORD and wept with many tears.

[11] Making a vow, she pleaded, "LORD of Armies, if you will take notice of your servant's affliction, remember and not forget me, and give your servant a son, I will give him to the LORD all the days of his life, and his hair will never be cut."

[12] While she continued praying in the LORD's presence, Eli watched her mouth. [13] Hannah was praying silently, and though her lips were moving, her voice could not be heard. Eli thought she was drunk [14] and said to her, "How long are you going to be drunk? Get rid of your wine!"

[15] "No, my lord," Hannah replied. "I am a woman with a broken heart. I haven't had any wine or beer; I've been pouring out my heart before the LORD. [16] Don't think of me as a wicked woman; I've been praying from the depth of my anguish and resentment."

[17] Eli responded, "Go in peace, and may the God of Israel grant the request you've made of him."

[18] "May your servant find favor with you," she replied. Then Hannah went on her way; she ate and no longer looked despondent.

SAMUEL'S BIRTH AND DEDICATION

[19] The next morning Elkanah and Hannah got up early to worship before the LORD. Afterward, they returned home to Ramah. Then Elkanah was intimate with his wife Hannah, and the LORD remembered her. [20] After some time, Hannah conceived and gave birth to a son. She named him Samuel, because she said, "I requested him from the LORD."

[21] When Elkanah and all his household went up to make the annual sacrifice and his vow offering to the LORD, [22] Hannah did not go and explained to her husband, "After the child is weaned, I'll take him to appear in the LORD's presence and to stay there permanently."

[23] Her husband, Elkanah, replied, "Do what you think is best, and stay here until you've weaned him. May the LORD confirm your word." So Hannah stayed there and nursed her son until she weaned him. [24] When she had weaned him, she took him with her to Shiloh, as well as a three-year-old bull, half a bushel of flour, and a clay jar of wine. Though the boy was still young, she took him to the LORD's house at Shiloh. [25] Then they slaughtered the bull and brought the boy to Eli.

²⁶ "Please, my lord," she said, "as surely as you live, my lord, I am the woman who stood here beside you praying to the Lᴏʀᴅ. ²⁷ I prayed for this boy, and

SINCE THE LORD GAVE ME WHAT I ASKED HIM FOR, ²⁸ I NOW GIVE THE BOY TO THE LORD. FOR AS LONG AS HE LIVES, HE IS GIVEN TO THE LORD."

Then he worshiped the Lᴏʀᴅ there.

1 SAMUEL 2:1-11

HANNAH'S TRIUMPHANT PRAYER

¹ Hannah prayed:

> My heart rejoices in the Lᴏʀᴅ;
> my horn is lifted up by the Lᴏʀᴅ.
> My mouth boasts over my enemies,
> because I rejoice in your salvation.
> ² There is no one holy like the Lᴏʀᴅ.
> There is no one besides you!
> And there is no rock like our God.
> ³ Do not boast so proudly,
> or let arrogant words come out of your mouth,
> for the Lᴏʀᴅ is a God of knowledge,
> and actions are weighed by him.
> ⁴ The bows of the warriors are broken,
> but the feeble are clothed with strength.
> ⁵ Those who are full hire themselves out for food,
> but those who are starving hunger no more.
> The woman who is childless gives birth to seven,
> but the woman with many sons pines away.
> ⁶ The Lᴏʀᴅ brings death and gives life;
> he sends some down to Sheol, and he raises others up.
> ⁷ The Lᴏʀᴅ brings poverty and gives wealth;
> he humbles and he exalts.
> ⁸ He raises the poor from the dust
> and lifts the needy from the trash heap.
> He seats them with noblemen

and gives them a throne of honor.
For the foundations of the earth are the Lord's;
he has set the world on them.
⁹ He guards the steps of his faithful ones,
but the wicked perish in darkness,
for a person does not prevail by his own strength.
¹⁰ Those who oppose the Lord will be shattered;
he will thunder in the heavens against them.
The Lord will judge the ends of the earth.
He will give power to his king;
he will lift up the horn of his anointed.

¹¹ Elkanah went home to Ramah, but the boy served the
Lord in the presence of the priest Eli.

RESPOND

01 WHERE DO I SEE GOD AT WORK IN HANNAH'S STORY?

_____
_____
_____
_____
_____
_____
_____
_____
_____
_____

02 HOW DO I CONNECT TO HANNAH'S EXPERIENCES? IN WHAT WAYS DO HER EXPERIENCES FEEL FOREIGN TO ME?

_____
_____
_____
_____
_____
_____
_____
_____
_____
_____

03 AFTER READING HANNAH'S STORY, WHAT DO I WANT TO CONTINUE TO MEDITATE ON?

_____
_____
_____
_____
_____
_____
_____
_____
_____

SAMUEL

THE PROPHET RAISED IN THE LORD'S HOUSE

1 SAMUEL 2:12–26

ELI'S FAMILY JUDGED

¹² Eli's sons were wicked men; they did not respect the LORD ¹³ or the priests' share of the sacrifices from the people. When anyone offered a sacrifice, the priest's servant would come with a three-pronged meat fork while the meat was boiling ¹⁴ and plunge it into the container, kettle, cauldron, or cooking pot. The priest would claim for himself whatever the meat fork brought up. This is the way they treated all the Israelites who came there to Shiloh. ¹⁵ Even before the fat was burned, the priest's servant would come and say to the one who was sacrificing, "Give the priest some meat to roast, because he won't accept boiled meat from you—only raw." ¹⁶ If that person said to him, "The fat must be burned first; then you can take whatever you want for yourself," the servant would reply, "No, I insist that you hand it over right now. If you don't, I'll take it by force!" ¹⁷ So the servants' sin was very severe in the presence of the LORD, because the men treated the LORD's offering with contempt.

18 Samuel served in the Lord's presence—this mere boy was dressed in the linen ephod. 19 Each year his mother made him a little robe and took it to him when she went with her husband to offer the annual sacrifice. 20 Eli would bless Elkanah and his wife: "May the Lord give you children by this woman in place of the one she has given to the Lord." Then they would go home.

21 The Lord paid attention to Hannah's need, and she conceived and gave birth to three sons and two daughters. Meanwhile, the boy Samuel grew up in the presence of the Lord.

22 Now Eli was very old. He heard about everything his sons were doing to all Israel and how they were sleeping with the women who served at the entrance to the tent of meeting. 23 He said to them, "Why are you doing these things? I have heard about your evil actions from all these people. 24 No, my sons, the news I hear the Lord's people spreading is not good. 25 If one person sins against another, God can intercede for him, but if a person sins against the Lord, who can intercede for him?" But they would not listen to their father, since the Lord intended to kill them. 26 By contrast, the boy Samuel grew in stature and in favor with the Lord and with people.

1 SAMUEL 3

SAMUEL'S CALL

1 The boy Samuel served the Lord in Eli's presence. In those days the word of the Lord was rare and prophetic visions were not widespread.

2 One day Eli, whose eyesight was failing, was lying in his usual place. 3 Before the lamp of God had gone out, Samuel was lying down in the temple of the Lord, where the ark of God was located.

4 Then the Lord called Samuel, and he answered, "Here I am." 5 He ran to Eli and said, "Here I am; you called me."

"I didn't call," Eli replied. "Go back and lie down." So he went and lay down.

6 Once again the Lord called, "Samuel!"

Samuel got up, went to Eli, and said, "Here I am; you called me."

"I didn't call, my son," he replied. "Go back and lie down."

7 Now Samuel did not yet know the Lord, because the word of the Lord had not yet been revealed to him. 8 Once again, for the third time, the Lord called Samuel. He got up, went to Eli, and said, "Here I am; you called me."

Then Eli understood that the Lord was calling the boy. 9 He told Samuel, "Go and lie down. If he calls you, say, 'Speak, Lord, for your servant is listening.'" So Samuel went and lay down in his place.

10 The Lord came, stood there, and called as before, "Samuel, Samuel!"

SAMUEL RESPONDED, "SPEAK, FOR YOUR SERVANT IS LISTENING."

11 The Lord said to Samuel, "I am about to do something in Israel that will cause everyone who hears about it to shudder. 12 On that day I will

carry out against Eli everything I said about his family, from beginning to end. [13] I told him that I am going to judge his family forever because of the iniquity he knows about: his sons are cursing God, and he has not stopped them. [14] Therefore, I have sworn to Eli's family: The iniquity of Eli's family will never be wiped out by either sacrifice or offering."

[15] Samuel lay down until the morning; then he opened the doors of the LORD's house. He was afraid to tell Eli the vision, [16] but Eli called him and said, "Samuel, my son."

"Here I am," answered Samuel.

[17] "What was the message he gave you?" Eli asked. "Don't hide it from me. May God punish you and do so severely if you hide anything from me that he told you." [18] So Samuel told him everything and did not hide anything from him. Eli responded, "He is the LORD. Let him do what he thinks is good."

[19] Samuel grew. The LORD was with him, and he fulfilled everything Samuel prophesied. [20] All Israel from Dan to Beer-sheba knew that Samuel was a confirmed prophet of the LORD. [21] The LORD continued to appear in Shiloh, because there he revealed himself to Samuel by his word.

1 SAMUEL 12:1–7, 13–25

SAMUEL'S FINAL PUBLIC SPEECH

[1] Then Samuel said to all Israel, "I have carefully listened to everything you said to me and placed a king over you. [2] Now you can see that the king is leading you. As for me, I'm old and gray, and my sons are here with you. I have led you from my youth until now. [3] Here I am. Bring charges against me before the LORD and his anointed: Whose ox or donkey have I taken? Who have I wronged or mistreated? Who gave me a bribe to overlook something? I will return it to you."

[4] "You haven't wronged us, you haven't mistreated us, and you haven't taken anything from anyone," they responded.

[5] He said to them, "The LORD is a witness against you, and his anointed is a witness today that you haven't found anything in my hand."

"He is a witness," they said.

⁶ Then Samuel said to the people, "The Lord, who appointed Moses and Aaron and who brought your ancestors up from the land of Egypt, is a witness. ⁷ Now present yourselves, so I may confront you before the Lord about all the righteous acts he has done for you and your ancestors."

. . .

¹³ "Now here is the king you've chosen, the one you requested. Look, this is the king the Lord has placed over you. ¹⁴ If you fear the Lord, worship and obey him, and if you don't rebel against the Lord's command, then both you and the king who reigns over you will follow the Lord your God. ¹⁵ However, if you disobey the Lord and rebel against his command, the Lord's hand will be against you as it was against your ancestors.

¹⁶ "Now, therefore, present yourselves and see this great thing that the Lord will do before your eyes. ¹⁷ Isn't the wheat harvest today? I will call on the Lord, and he will send thunder and rain so that you will recognize what an immense evil you committed in the Lord's sight by requesting a king for yourselves." ¹⁸ Samuel called on the Lord, and on that day the Lord sent thunder and rain. As a result, all the people greatly feared the Lord and Samuel.

¹⁹ They pleaded with Samuel, "Pray to the Lord your God for your servants so we won't die! For we have added to all our sins the evil of requesting a king for ourselves."

²⁰ Samuel replied, "Don't be afraid. Even though you have committed all this evil, don't turn away from following the Lord. Instead, worship the Lord with all your heart. ²¹ Don't turn away to follow worthless things that can't profit or rescue you; they are worthless. ²² The Lord will not abandon his people, because of his great name and because he has determined to make you his own people.

²³ "As for me, I vow that I will not sin against the Lord by ceasing to pray for you. I will teach you the good and right way. ²⁴ Above all, fear the Lord and worship him faithfully with all your heart; consider the great things he has done for you. ²⁵ However, if you continue to do what is evil, both you and your king will be swept away."

RESPOND

01 WHERE DO I SEE GOD AT WORK IN
SAMUEL'S STORY?

_____
_____
_____
_____
_____
_____
_____
_____
_____
_____

02 HOW DO I CONNECT TO SAMUEL'S
EXPERIENCES? IN WHAT WAYS DO HIS
EXPERIENCES FEEL FOREIGN TO ME?

_____
_____
_____
_____
_____
_____
_____
_____
_____
_____

_____

03 AFTER READING SAMUEL'S STORY, WHAT DO I WANT TO CONTINUE TO MEDITATE ON?

_____
_____
_____
_____
_____
_____
_____
_____
_____

SAUL

THE FIRST KING OF ISRAEL

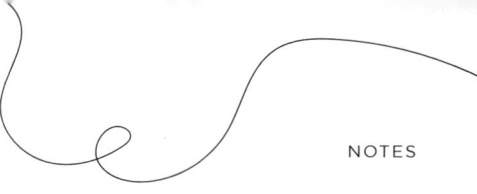

SAUL ANOINTED KING

¹ There was a prominent man of Benjamin named Kish son of Abiel, son of Zeror, son of Becorath, son of Aphiah, son of a Benjaminite. ² He had a son named Saul, an impressive young man. There was no one more impressive among the Israelites than he. He stood a head taller than anyone else.

. . .

¹⁷ When Samuel saw Saul, the LORD told him, "Here is the man I told you about; he will govern my people."

¹⁸ Saul approached Samuel in the city gate and asked, "Would you please tell me where the seer's house is?"

¹⁹ "I am the seer," Samuel answered. "Go up ahead of me to the high place and eat with me today. When I send you off in the morning, I'll tell you everything that's in your heart."

. . .

²⁶ They got up early, and just before dawn, Samuel called to Saul on the roof, "Get up, and I'll send you on your way!" Saul got up, and both he and Samuel went outside. ²⁷ As they were going down to the edge of the city, Samuel said to Saul, "Tell the servant to go on ahead of us, but you stay for a while, and I'll reveal the word of God to you." So the servant went on.

1 SAMUEL 10:1-10, 17-24

¹ Samuel took the flask of oil, poured it out on Saul's head, kissed him, and said, "Hasn't the LORD anointed you ruler over his inheritance? ² Today when you leave me, you'll find two men at Rachel's Grave at Zelzah in the territory of Benjamin. They will say to you, 'The donkeys you went looking for have been found, and now your father has stopped being concerned about the donkeys and is worried about you, asking: What should I do about my son?'

³ "You will proceed from there until you come to the oak of Tabor. Three men going up to God at Bethel will meet you there, one bringing three goats, one bringing three loaves of bread, and one bringing a clay jar of wine. ⁴ They will ask how you are and give you two loaves of bread, which you will accept from them.

5 "After that you will come to Gibeah of God where there are Philistine garrisons. When you arrive at the city, you will meet a group of prophets coming down from the high place prophesying. They will be preceded by harps, tambourines, flutes, and lyres. 6 The Spirit of the LORD will come powerfully on you, you will prophesy with them, and you will be transformed. 7 When these signs have happened to you, do whatever your circumstances require because God is with you. 8 Afterward, go ahead of me to Gilgal. I will come to you to offer burnt offerings and to sacrifice fellowship offerings. Wait seven days until I come to you and show you what to do."

9 When Saul turned to leave Samuel, God changed his heart, and all the signs came about that day. 10 When Saul and his servant arrived at Gibeah, a group of prophets met him. Then the Spirit of God came powerfully on him, and he prophesied along with them.

…

SAUL RECEIVED AS KING

17 Samuel summoned the people to the LORD at Mizpah 18 and said to the Israelites, "This is what the LORD, the God of Israel, says: 'I brought Israel out of Egypt, and I rescued you from the power of the Egyptians and all the kingdoms that were oppressing you.' 19 But today you have rejected your God, who saves you from all your troubles and afflictions. You said to him, 'You must set a king over us.' Now therefore present yourselves before the LORD by your tribes and clans."

20 Samuel had all the tribes of Israel come forward, and the tribe of Benjamin was selected. 21 Then he had the tribe of Benjamin come forward by its clans, and the Matrite clan was selected. Finally, Saul son of Kish was selected. But when they searched for him, they could not find him. 22 They again inquired of the LORD, "Has the man come here yet?"

The LORD replied, "There he is, hidden among the supplies."

23 They ran and got him from there. When he stood among the people, he stood a head taller than anyone else. 24 Samuel said to all the people, "Do you see the one the LORD has chosen? There is no one like him among the entire population."

And all the people shouted, "Long live the king!"

1 SAMUEL 15:1-29, 34-35

SAUL REJECTED AS KING

1 Samuel told Saul, "The LORD sent me to anoint you as king over his people Israel. Now, listen to the words of the LORD. 2 This is what the LORD of Armies says: 'I witnessed what the Amalekites did to the Israelites when they opposed them along the way as they were coming out of Egypt. 3 Now go and attack the Amalekites and completely destroy everything they have. Do not spare them. Kill men and women, infants and nursing babies, oxen and sheep, camels and donkeys.'"

4 Then Saul summoned the troops and counted them at Telaim: two hundred thousand foot soldiers and ten thousand men from Judah. 5 Saul came to the city of Amalek and set up an ambush in the wadi. 6 He warned the Kenites, "Since you showed kindness to all the Israelites when they came out of Egypt, go on and leave! Get away from the Amalekites, or I'll sweep you away with them." So the Kenites withdrew from the Amalekites.

7 Then Saul struck down the Amalekites from Havilah all the way to Shur, which is next to Egypt. 8 He captured King Agag of Amalek alive, but he completely destroyed all the rest of the people with the sword. 9 Saul and the troops spared Agag, and the best of the sheep, goats, cattle, and choice animals, as well as the young rams and the best of everything else. They were not willing to destroy them, but they did destroy all the worthless and unwanted things.

10 Then the word of the LORD came to Samuel,

11 "I REGRET THAT I MADE SAUL KING, FOR HE HAS TURNED AWAY FROM FOLLOWING ME AND HAS NOT CARRIED OUT MY INSTRUCTIONS."

So Samuel became angry and cried out to the LORD all night.

12 Early in the morning Samuel got up to confront Saul, but it was reported to Samuel, "Saul went to Carmel where he set up a monument for himself. Then he turned around and went down to Gilgal." 13 When Samuel came to him, Saul said, "May the LORD bless you. I have carried out the LORD's instructions."

14 Samuel replied, "Then what is this sound of sheep, goats, and cattle I hear?"

15 Saul answered, "The troops brought them from the Amalekites and spared the best sheep, goats, and cattle in order to offer a sacrifice to the LORD your God, but the rest we destroyed."

16 "Stop!" exclaimed Samuel. "Let me tell you what the LORD said to me last night."

"Tell me," he replied.

17 Samuel continued, "Although you once considered yourself unimportant, haven't you become the leader of the tribes of Israel? The LORD anointed you king over Israel 18 and then sent you on a mission and said, 'Go and completely destroy the sinful Amalekites. Fight against them until you have annihilated them.' 19 So why didn't you obey the LORD? Why did you rush on the plunder and do what was evil in the LORD's sight?"

²⁰ "But I did obey the Lord!" Saul answered. "I went on the mission the Lord gave me: I brought back King Agag of Amalek, and I completely destroyed the Amalekites. ²¹ The troops took sheep, goats, and cattle from the plunder—the best of what was set apart for destruction—to sacrifice to the Lord your God at Gilgal."

²² Then Samuel said:

> Does the Lord take pleasure in burnt offerings and sacrifices
> as much as in obeying the Lord?
> Look: to obey is better than sacrifice,
> to pay attention is better than the fat of rams.
> ²³ For rebellion is like the sin of divination,
> and defiance is like wickedness and idolatry.
> Because you have rejected the word of the Lord,
> he has rejected you as king.

²⁴ Saul answered Samuel, "I have sinned. I have transgressed the Lord's command and your words. Because I was afraid of the people, I obeyed them. ²⁵ Now therefore, please forgive my sin and return with me so I can worship the Lord."

²⁶ Samuel replied to Saul, "I will not return with you. Because you rejected the word of the Lord, the Lord has rejected you from being king over Israel." ²⁷ When Samuel turned to go, Saul grabbed the corner of his robe, and it tore. ²⁸ Samuel said to him, "The Lord has torn the kingship of Israel away from you today and has given it to your neighbor who is better than you. ²⁹ Furthermore, the Eternal One of Israel does not lie or change his mind, for he is not man who changes his mind."

...

³⁴ Samuel went to Ramah, and Saul went up to his home in Gibeah of Saul. ³⁵ Even to the day of his death, Samuel never saw Saul again. Samuel mourned for Saul, and the Lord regretted he had made Saul king over Israel.

RESPOND

01 WHERE DO I SEE GOD AT WORK IN
SAUL'S STORY?

_____
_____
_____
_____
_____
_____
_____
_____
_____

02 HOW DO I CONNECT TO SAUL'S
EXPERIENCES? IN WHAT WAYS DO HIS
EXPERIENCES FEEL FOREIGN TO ME?

_____
_____
_____
_____
_____
_____
_____
_____
_____

03 AFTER READING SAUL'S STORY, WHAT DO I WANT TO CONTINUE TO MEDITATE ON?

_____
_____
_____
_____
_____
_____
_____
_____

GRACE DAY

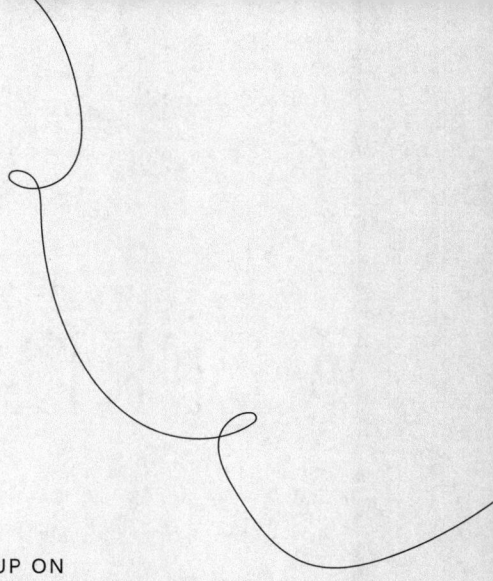

TAKE THIS DAY TO CATCH UP ON
YOUR READING, PRAY, AND REST IN
THE PRESENCE OF THE LORD.

NOW IN A LARGE HOUSE THERE ARE
NOT ONLY GOLD AND SILVER VESSELS,
BUT ALSO THOSE OF WOOD AND CLAY;
SOME FOR HONORABLE USE AND SOME
FOR DISHONORABLE. SO IF ANYONE
PURIFIES HIMSELF FROM ANYTHING
DISHONORABLE, HE WILL BE A SPECIAL
INSTRUMENT, SET APART, USEFUL TO
THE MASTER, PREPARED FOR EVERY
GOOD WORK.

2 TIMOTHY 2:20–21

WEEKLY

SCRIPTURE IS GOD BREATHED AND TRUE.
WHEN WE MEMORIZE IT, WE CARRY THE GOOD
NEWS OF JESUS WITH US WHEREVER WE GO.

FOR THIS PLAN, WE ARE MEMORIZING OUR KEY
PASSAGE, PSALM 8:3–4. WE WILL CONTINUE
WITH THE FOURTH LINE.

SEE TIPS FOR MEMORIZING SCRIPTURE ON PAGE 236.

TRUTH

PSALM 8:3–4

WHEN I OBSERVE YOUR HEAVENS,
THE WORK OF YOUR FINGERS,
THE MOON AND THE STARS,
WHICH YOU SET IN PLACE,
WHAT IS A HUMAN BEING THAT YOU REMEMBER HIM,
A SON OF MAN THAT YOU LOOK AFTER HIM?

DAVID

AN ANOINTED SHEPHERD AND KING OVER ISRAEL

1 SAMUEL 16:1-13

SAMUEL ANOINTS DAVID

¹ The LORD said to Samuel, "How long are you going to mourn for Saul, since I have rejected him as king over Israel? Fill your horn with oil and go. I am sending you to Jesse of Bethlehem because I have selected for myself a king from his sons."

² Samuel asked, "How can I go? Saul will hear about it and kill me!"

The LORD answered, "Take a young cow with you and say, 'I have come to sacrifice to the LORD.' ³ Then invite Jesse to the sacrifice, and I will let you know what you are to do. You are to anoint for me the one I indicate to you."

⁴ Samuel did what the LORD directed and went to Bethlehem. When the elders of the town met him, they trembled and asked, "Do you come in peace?"

⁵ "In peace," he replied. "I've come to sacrifice to the LORD. Consecrate yourselves and come

with me to the sacrifice." Then he consecrated Jesse and his sons and invited them to the sacrifice. ⁶ When they arrived, Samuel saw Eliab and said, "Certainly the LORD's anointed one is here before him."

⁷ But the LORD said to Samuel, "Do not look at his appearance or his stature because I have rejected him. Humans do not see what the LORD sees, for humans see what is visible, but the LORD sees the heart."

⁸ Jesse called Abinadab and presented him to Samuel. "The LORD hasn't chosen this one either," Samuel said. ⁹ Then Jesse presented Shammah, but Samuel said, "The LORD hasn't chosen this one either." ¹⁰ After Jesse presented seven of his sons to him, Samuel told Jesse, "The LORD hasn't chosen any of these." ¹¹ Samuel asked him, "Are these all the sons you have?"

"There is still the youngest," he answered, "but right now he's tending the sheep." Samuel told

Jesse, "Send for him. We won't sit down to eat until he gets here." [12] So Jesse sent for him. He had beautiful eyes and a healthy, handsome appearance.

Then the LORD said, "Anoint him, for he is the one." [13] So Samuel took the horn of oil and anointed him in the presence of his brothers, and the Spirit of the LORD came powerfully on David from that day forward. Then Samuel set out and went to Ramah.

2 SAMUEL 5:1-5, 9-12

DAVID, KING OF ISRAEL

[1] All the tribes of Israel came to David at Hebron and said, "Here we are, your own flesh and blood. [2] Even while Saul was king over us, you were the one who led us out to battle and brought us back. The LORD also said to you, 'You will shepherd my people Israel, and you will be ruler over Israel.'"

[3] So all the elders of Israel came to the king at Hebron. King David made a covenant with them at Hebron in the LORD's presence, and they anointed David king over Israel.

[4] David was thirty years old when he began his reign; he reigned forty years. [5] In Hebron he reigned over Judah seven years and six months, and in Jerusalem he reigned thirty-three years over all Israel and Judah.

. . .

[9] David took up residence in the stronghold, which he named the city of David. He built it up all the way around from the supporting terraces inward. [10] David became more and more powerful,

AND THE LORD GOD OF ARMIES WAS WITH HIM.

[11] King Hiram of Tyre sent envoys to David; he also sent cedar logs, carpenters, and stonemasons, and they built a palace for David. [12] Then David knew that the LORD had established him as king over Israel and had exalted his kingdom for the sake of his people Israel.

THE LORD'S COVENANT WITH DAVID

¹ When the king had settled into his palace and the LORD had given him rest on every side from all his enemies, ² the king said to the prophet Nathan, "Look, I am living in a cedar house while the ark of God sits inside tent curtains."

³ So Nathan told the king, "Go and do all that is on your mind, for the LORD is with you."

⁴ But that night the word of the LORD came to Nathan: ⁵ "Go to my servant David and say, 'This is what the LORD says: Are you to build me a house to dwell in? ⁶ From the time I brought the Israelites out of Egypt until today I have not dwelt in a house; instead, I have been moving around with a tent as my dwelling. ⁷ In all my journeys with all the Israelites, have I ever spoken a word to one of the tribal leaders of Israel, whom I commanded to shepherd my people Israel, asking: Why haven't you built me a house of cedar?'

⁸ "So now this is what you are to say to my servant David: 'This is what the LORD of Armies says: I took you from the pasture, from tending the flock, to be ruler over my people Israel. ⁹ I have been with you wherever you have gone, and I have destroyed all your enemies before you. I will make a great name for you like that of the greatest on the earth. ¹⁰ I will designate a place for my people Israel and plant them, so that they may live there and not be disturbed again. Evildoers will not continue to oppress them as they have done ¹¹ ever since the day I ordered judges to be over my people Israel. I will give you rest from all your enemies.

"'The LORD declares to you: The LORD himself will make a house for you. ¹² When your time comes and you rest with your ancestors, I will raise up after you your descendant, who will come from your body, and I will establish his kingdom. ¹³ He is the one who will build a house for my name, and I will establish the throne of his kingdom forever. ¹⁴ I will be his father, and he will be my son. When he does wrong, I will discipline him with a rod of men and blows from mortals. ¹⁵ But my faithful love will never leave him as it did when I removed it from Saul, whom I removed from before you. ¹⁶ Your house and kingdom will endure before me forever, and your throne will be established forever.'"

¹⁷ Nathan reported all these words and this entire vision to David.

DAVID'S PRAYER OF THANKSGIVING

¹⁸ Then King David went in, sat in the LORD's presence, and said,

Who am I, Lord GOD, and what is my house that you have brought me this far? ¹⁹ What you have done so far was a little thing to you, Lord GOD, for you have also spoken about your servant's house in the distant future. And this is a revelation for mankind, Lord GOD. ²⁰ What more can David say to you? You know your servant, Lord GOD. ²¹ Because of your word and according to your will, you have revealed all these great things to your servant.

²² This is why you are great, Lord GOD. There is no one like you, and there is no God besides you, as all we have heard confirms. ²³ And who is like your people Israel? God came to one nation on earth in order to redeem a people for himself, to make a name for himself, and to perform for them great and awesome acts, driving out nations and their gods before your people you redeemed for yourself from Egypt. ²⁴ You established your people Israel to be your own people forever, and you, LORD, have become their God.

²⁵ Now, LORD God, fulfill the promise forever that you have made to your servant and his house. Do as you have promised, ²⁶ so that your name will be exalted forever, when it is said, "The LORD of Armies is God over Israel." The house of your servant David will be established before you ²⁷ since you, LORD of Armies, God of Israel, have revealed this to your servant when you said, "I will build a house for you." Therefore, your servant has found the courage to pray this prayer to you. ²⁸ Lord GOD, you are God; your words are true, and you have promised this good thing to your servant. ²⁹ Now, please bless your servant's house so that it will continue before you forever. For you, Lord GOD, have spoken, and with your blessing your servant's house will be blessed forever.

RESPOND

1. WHERE DO I SEE GOD AT WORK IN DAVID'S STORY?

2. HOW DO I CONNECT TO DAVID'S EXPERIENCES? IN WHAT WAYS DO HIS EXPERIENCES FEEL FOREIGN TO ME?

3. AFTER READING DAVID'S STORY, WHAT DO I WANT TO CONTINUE TO MEDITATE ON?

ABIGAIL

1 SAMUEL 25

DAVID, NABAL, AND ABIGAIL

¹ Samuel died, and all Israel assembled to mourn for him, and they buried him by his home in Ramah. David then went down to the Wilderness of Paran.

² A man in Maon had a business in Carmel; he was a very rich man with three thousand sheep and one thousand goats and was shearing his sheep in Carmel. ³ The man's name was Nabal, and his wife's name, Abigail. The woman was intelligent and beautiful, but the man, a Calebite, was harsh and evil in his dealings.

⁴ While David was in the wilderness, he heard that Nabal was shearing sheep, ⁵ so David sent ten young men instructing them, "Go up to Carmel, and when you come to Nabal, greet him in my name. ⁶ Then say this: 'Long life to you, and peace to you, peace to your family, and peace to all that is yours. ⁷ I hear that you are shearing. When your shepherds were with us, we did not harass them, and nothing of theirs was missing the whole time they were in Carmel. ⁸ Ask your young men, and they will tell you. So let my young men find favor with you, for we have come on a feast day. Please give whatever you have on hand to your servants and to your son David.'"

⁹ David's young men went and said all these things to Nabal on David's behalf, and they waited. ¹⁰ Nabal asked them, "Who is David? Who is Jesse's son? Many slaves these days are running away from their masters. ¹¹ Am I supposed to take my bread, my water, and my meat that I butchered for my shearers and give them to these men? I don't know where they are from."

¹² David's young men retraced their steps. When they returned to him, they reported all these words. ¹³ He said to his men, "All of you, put on your swords!" So each man put on his sword, and David also put on his sword. About four hundred men followed David while two hundred stayed with the supplies.

¹⁴ One of Nabal's young men informed Abigail, Nabal's wife, "Look, David sent messengers from the wilderness to greet our master, but he screamed at them. ¹⁵ The men treated us very well. When we were in the field, we weren't harassed and nothing of ours was missing the whole time we were living among them. ¹⁶ They were a wall around us, both day and night, the entire time we were with them herding the sheep. ¹⁷ Now consider carefully what you

should do, because there is certain to be trouble for our master and his entire family. He is such a worthless fool nobody can talk to him!"

[18] Abigail hurried, taking two hundred loaves of bread, two clay jars of wine, five butchered sheep, a bushel of roasted grain, one hundred clusters of raisins, and two hundred cakes of pressed figs, and loaded them on donkeys. [19] Then she said to her male servants, "Go ahead of me. I will be right behind you." But she did not tell her husband, Nabal.

[20] As she rode the donkey down a mountain pass hidden from view, she saw David and his men coming toward her and met them. [21] David had just said, "I guarded everything that belonged to this man in the wilderness for nothing. He was not missing anything, yet he paid me back evil for good. [22] May God punish me and do so severely if I let any of his males survive until morning."

[23] When Abigail saw David, she quickly got off the donkey and knelt down with her face to the ground and paid homage to David. [24] She knelt at his feet and said, "The guilt is mine, my lord, but please let your servant speak to you directly. Listen to the words of your servant. [25] My lord should pay no attention to this worthless fool Nabal, for he lives up to his name: His name means 'stupid,' and stupidity is all he knows. I, your servant, didn't see my lord's young men whom you sent. [26] Now my lord, as surely as the LORD lives and as you yourself live—it is the LORD who kept you from participating in bloodshed and avenging yourself by your own hand—may your enemies and those who intend to harm my lord be like Nabal. [27] Let this gift your servant has brought to my lord be given to the young men who follow my lord. [28] Please forgive your servant's offense, for the LORD is certain to make a lasting dynasty for my lord because he fights the LORD's battles. Throughout your life, may evil not be found in you.

[29] "Someone is pursuing you and intends to take your life. My lord's life is tucked safely in the place where the LORD your God protects the living, but he is flinging away your enemies' lives like stones from a sling. [30] When the LORD does for my lord all the good he promised you and appoints you ruler over Israel, [31] there will not be remorse or a troubled conscience for my lord because of needless bloodshed or my lord's revenge. And when the LORD does good things for my lord, may you remember me your servant."

^{32} Then David said to Abigail, "Blessed be the LORD God of Israel, who sent you to meet me today! ^{33} May your discernment be blessed, and may you be blessed. Today you kept me from participating in bloodshed and avenging myself by my own hand. ^{34} Otherwise, as surely as the LORD God of Israel lives, who prevented me from harming you, if you had not come quickly to meet me, Nabal wouldn't have had any males left by morning light." ^{35} Then David accepted what she had brought him and said, "Go home in peace. See, I have heard what you said and have granted your request."

^{36} Then Abigail went to Nabal, and there he was in his house, holding a feast fit for a king. Nabal's heart was cheerful, and he was very drunk, so she didn't say anything to him until morning light.

^{37} In the morning when Nabal sobered up, his wife told him about these events. His heart died and he became a stone. ^{38} About ten days later, the LORD struck Nabal dead.

^{39} When David heard that Nabal was dead, he said, "Blessed be the LORD who championed my cause against Nabal's insults and restrained his servant from doing evil. The LORD brought Nabal's evil deeds back on his own head."

Then David sent messengers to speak to Abigail about marrying him. ^{40} When David's servants came to Abigail at Carmel, they said to her, "David sent us to bring you to him as a wife."

^{41} She stood up, paid homage with her face to the ground, and said, "Here I am, your servant, a slave to wash the feet of my lord's servants." ^{42} Then Abigail got up quickly, and with her five female servants accompanying her, rode on the donkey following David's messengers. And so she became his wife.

^{43} David also married Ahinoam of Jezreel, and the two of them became his wives. ^{44} But Saul gave his daughter Michal, David's wife, to Palti son of Laish, who was from Gallim.

RESPOND

DATE   /   /

1.
WHERE DO I SEE GOD AT WORK IN ABIGAIL'S STORY?

2.
HOW DO I CONNECT TO ABIGAIL'S EXPERIENCES? IN WHAT WAYS DO HER EXPERIENCES FEEL FOREIGN TO ME?

3.
AFTER READING ABIGAIL'S STORY, WHAT DO I WANT TO CONTINUE TO MEDITATE ON?

MEPHIBOSHETH
A RECIPIENT OF THE KING'S KINDNESS

2 SAMUEL 4:4

Saul's son Jonathan had a son whose feet were crippled. He was five years old when the report about Saul and Jonathan came from Jezreel. His nanny picked him up and fled, but as she was hurrying to flee, he fell and became lame. His name was Mephibosheth.

2 SAMUEL 9

DAVID'S KINDNESS TO MEPHIBOSHETH

¹ David asked, "Is there anyone remaining from the family of Saul I can show kindness to for Jonathan's sake?" ² There was a servant of Saul's family named Ziba. They summoned him to David, and the king said to him, "Are you Ziba?"

"I am your servant," he replied.

³ So the king asked, "Is there anyone left of Saul's family that I can show the kindness of God to?"

Ziba said to the king, "There is still Jonathan's son who was injured in both feet."

⁴ The king asked him, "Where is he?"

Ziba answered the king, "You'll find him in Lo-debar at the house of Machir son of Ammiel." ⁵ So King David had him brought from the house of Machir son of Ammiel in Lo-debar.

⁶ Mephibosheth son of Jonathan son of Saul came to David, fell facedown, and paid homage. David said, "Mephibosheth!"

"I am your servant," he replied.

⁷ "Don't be afraid," David said to him, "since I intend to show you kindness for the sake of your father Jonathan. I will restore to you all your grandfather Saul's fields, and you will always eat meals at my table."

⁸ Mephibosheth paid homage and said, "What is your servant that you take an interest in a dead dog like me?"

⁹ Then the king summoned Saul's attendant Ziba and said to him, "I have given to your master's grandson all that belonged to Saul and his family. ¹⁰ You, your sons, and your servants are to work the ground for him, and you are to bring in the crops so your master's grandson will have food to eat. But Mephibosheth, your master's grandson, is always to eat at my table." Now Ziba had fifteen sons and twenty servants.

¹¹ Ziba said to the king, "Your servant will do all my lord the king commands."

SO MEPHIBOSHETH ATE AT DAVID'S TABLE JUST LIKE ONE OF THE KING'S SONS.

¹² Mephibosheth had a young son whose name was Mica. All those living in Ziba's house were Mephibosheth's servants. ¹³ However, Mephibosheth lived in Jerusalem because he always ate at the king's table. His feet had been injured.

RESPOND

1. WHERE DO I SEE GOD AT WORK IN MEPHIBOSHETH'S STORY?

2. HOW DO I CONNECT TO MEPHIBOSHETH'S EXPERIENCES? IN WHAT WAYS DO HIS EXPERIENCES FEEL FOREIGN TO ME?

3. AFTER READING MEPHIBOSHETH'S STORY, WHAT DO I WANT TO CONTINUE TO MEDITATE ON?

BATHSHEBA

DAY 32 ⌒⌒⌒⌒⌒ WEEK 5

2 SAMUEL 11:1-17, 26-27

DAVID'S ADULTERY WITH BATHSHEBA

¹ In the spring when kings march out to war, David sent Joab with his officers and all Israel. They destroyed the Ammonites and besieged Rabbah, but David remained in Jerusalem.

² One evening David got up from his bed and strolled around on the roof of the palace. From the roof he saw a woman bathing—a very beautiful woman. ³ So David sent someone to inquire about her, and he said, "Isn't this Bathsheba, daughter of Eliam and wife of Uriah the Hethite?"

⁴ David sent messengers to get her, and when she came to him, he slept with her. Now she had just been purifying herself from her uncleanness. Afterward, she returned home. ⁵ The woman conceived and sent word to inform David, "I am pregnant."

⁶ David sent orders to Joab: "Send me Uriah the Hethite." So Joab sent Uriah to David. ⁷ When Uriah came to him, David asked how Joab and the troops were doing and how the war was going. ⁸ Then he said to Uriah, "Go down to your house and wash your feet." So Uriah left the palace, and a gift from the king followed him. ⁹ But Uriah slept at the door of the palace with all his master's servants; he did not go down to his house.

¹⁰ When it was reported to David, "Uriah didn't go home," David questioned Uriah, "Haven't you just come from a journey? Why didn't you go home?"

¹¹ Uriah answered David, "The ark, Israel, and Judah are dwelling in tents, and my master Joab and his soldiers are camping in the open field. How can I enter my house to eat and drink and sleep with my wife? As surely as you live and by your life, I will not do this!"

¹² "Stay here today also," David said to Uriah, "and tomorrow I will send you back." So Uriah stayed in Jerusalem that day and the next. ¹³ Then David invited Uriah to eat and drink with him, and David got him drunk. He went out in the evening to lie down on his cot with his master's servants, but he did not go home.

URIAH'S DEATH ARRANGED

¹⁴ The next morning David wrote a letter to Joab and sent it with Uriah. ¹⁵ In the letter he wrote:

Put Uriah at the front of the fiercest fighting, then withdraw from him so that he is struck down and dies.

¹⁶ When Joab was besieging the city, he put Uriah in the place where he knew the best enemy soldiers were. ¹⁷ Then the men of the city came out and attacked Joab, and some of the men from David's soldiers fell in battle; Uriah the Hethite also died.

. . .

²⁶ When Uriah's wife heard that her husband, Uriah, had died, she mourned for him. ²⁷ When the time of mourning ended, David had her brought to his house. She became his wife and bore him a son. However, the LORD considered what David had done to be evil.

2 SAMUEL 12:7-25

⁷ Nathan replied to David, "You are the man! This is what the LORD God of Israel says: 'I anointed you king over Israel, and I rescued you from Saul. ⁸ I gave your master's house to you and your master's wives into your arms, and I gave you the house of Israel and Judah, and if that was not enough, I would have given you even more. ⁹ Why then have you despised the LORD's command by doing what I consider evil? You struck down Uriah the Hethite with the sword and took his wife as your own wife—you murdered him with the Ammonite's sword. ¹⁰ Now therefore, the sword will never leave your house because you despised me and took the wife of Uriah the Hethite to be your own wife.'

¹¹ "This is what the LORD says, 'I am going to bring disaster on you from your own family: I will take your wives and give them to another before your very eyes, and he will sleep with them in broad daylight. ¹² You acted in secret, but I will do this before all Israel and in broad daylight.'"

¹³ David responded to Nathan, "I have sinned against the LORD."

Then Nathan replied to David, "And the LORD has taken away your sin; you will not die. ¹⁴ However, because you treated the LORD with such contempt in this matter, the son born to you will die." ¹⁵ Then Nathan went home.

THE DEATH OF BATHSHEBA'S SON

The LORD struck the baby that Uriah's wife had borne to David, and he became deathly ill. ¹⁶ David pleaded with God for the boy. He fasted, went home, and spent the night lying on the ground. [17] The elders of his house stood beside him to get him up from the ground, but he was unwilling and would not eat anything with them.

[18] On the seventh day the baby died. But David's servants were afraid to tell him the baby was dead. They said, "Look, while the baby was alive, we spoke to him, and he wouldn't listen to us. So how can we tell him the baby is dead? He may do something desperate."

[19] When David saw that his servants were whispering to each other, he guessed that the baby was dead. So he asked his servants, "Is the baby dead?"

"He is dead," they replied.

[20] Then David got up from the ground. He washed, anointed himself, changed his clothes, went to the LORD's house, and worshiped. Then he went home and requested something to eat. So they served him food, and he ate.

[21] His servants asked him, "Why have you done this? While the baby was alive, you fasted and wept, but when he died, you got up and ate food."

[22] He answered, "While the baby was alive, I fasted and wept because I thought, 'Who knows? The LORD may be gracious to me and let him live.' [23] But now that he is dead, why should I fast? Can I bring him back again? I'll go to him, but he will never return to me."

THE BIRTH OF SOLOMON

[24] Then David comforted his wife Bathsheba; he went to her and slept with her. She gave birth to a son and named him Solomon. The LORD loved him, [25] and he sent a message through the prophet Nathan, who named him Jedidiah, because of the LORD.

1 KINGS 1:5–31

ADONIJAH'S BID FOR POWER

[5] Adonijah son of Haggith kept exalting himself, saying, "I will be king!" He prepared chariots, cavalry, and fifty men to run ahead of him. [6] But his father had never once infuriated him by asking, "Why did you do that?" In addition, he was quite handsome and was born after Absalom.

[7] He conspired with Joab son of Zeruiah and with the priest Abiathar. They supported Adonijah, [8] but the priest Zadok, Benaiah son of Jehoiada, the prophet Nathan, Shimei, Rei, and David's royal guard did not side with Adonijah.

[9] Adonijah sacrificed sheep, goats, cattle, and fattened cattle near the stone of Zoheleth, which is next to En-rogel. He invited all his royal brothers and all the men of Judah, the servants of the king, [10] but he did not invite the prophet Nathan, Benaiah, the royal guard, or his brother Solomon.

NATHAN'S AND BATHSHEBA'S APPEALS

[11] Then Nathan said to Bathsheba, Solomon's mother, "Have you not heard that Adonijah son of Haggith has become king and our lord David does not know it? [12] Now please come and let me advise you. Save your life and the life of your son Solomon. [13] Go, approach King David and say to him, 'My lord the king, did you not swear to your servant: Your son Solomon is to become king after me, and he is the one who is to sit on my throne? So why has Adonijah become king?' [14] At that moment, while you are still there speaking with the king, I'll come in after you and confirm your words."

[15] So Bathsheba went to the king in his bedroom. Since the king was very old, Abishag the Shunammite was attending to him. [16] Bathsheba knelt low and paid homage to the king, and he asked, "What do you want?"

[17] She replied,

"MY LORD, YOU SWORE TO YOUR SERVANT BY THE LORD YOUR GOD, 'YOUR SON SOLOMON IS TO BECOME KING AFTER ME, AND HE IS THE ONE WHO IS TO SIT ON MY THRONE.'

[18] Now look, Adonijah has become king. And, my lord the king, you didn't know it. [19] He has lavishly sacrificed oxen, fattened cattle, and sheep. He invited all the king's sons, the priest Abiathar, and Joab the commander of the army, but he did not invite your servant Solomon. [20] Now, my lord the king, the eyes of all Israel are on you to tell them who will sit on the throne of my lord the king after him. [21] Otherwise, when my lord the king rests with his ancestors, I and my son Solomon will be regarded as criminals."

²² At that moment, while she was still speaking with the king, the prophet Nathan arrived, ²³ and it was announced to the king, "The prophet Nathan is here." He came into the king's presence and paid homage to him with his face to the ground.

²⁴ "My lord the king," Nathan said, "did you say, 'Adonijah is to become king after me, and he is the one who is to sit on my throne'? ²⁵ For today he went down and lavishly sacrificed oxen, fattened cattle, and sheep. He invited all the sons of the king, the commanders of the army, and the priest Abiathar. And look! They're eating and drinking in his presence, and they're saying, 'Long live King Adonijah!' ²⁶ But he did not invite me—me, your servant—or the priest Zadok or Benaiah son of Jehoiada or your servant Solomon. ²⁷ I'm certain my lord the king would not have let this happen without letting your servant know who will sit on my lord the king's throne after him."

SOLOMON CONFIRMED KING

²⁸ King David responded by saying, "Call in Bathsheba for me." So she came into the king's presence and stood before him. ²⁹ The king swore an oath and said, "As the LORD lives, who has redeemed my life from every difficulty, ³⁰ just as I swore to you by the LORD God of Israel: Your son Solomon is to become king after me, and he is the one who is to sit on my throne in my place, that is exactly what I will do this very day."

³¹ Bathsheba knelt low with her face to the ground, paying homage to the king, and said, "May my lord King David live forever!"

RESPOND

1. WHERE DO I SEE GOD AT WORK IN BATHSHEBA'S STORY?

2. HOW DO I CONNECT TO BATHSHEBA'S EXPERIENCES? IN WHAT WAYS DO HER EXPERIENCES FEEL FOREIGN TO ME?

3. AFTER READING BATHSHEBA'S STORY, WHAT DO I WANT TO CONTINUE TO MEDITATE ON?

SOLOMON

THE KING WHO SOUGHT AND RECEIVED WISDOM

SO GIVE YOUR SERVANT A RECEPTIVE HEART TO
JUDGE YOUR PEOPLE AND TO DISCERN BETWEEN GOOD
AND EVIL. FOR WHO IS ABLE TO JUDGE THIS GREAT
PEOPLE OF YOURS? —1 KINGS 3:9

DAY 33   WEEK 5

DAVID'S DYING INSTRUCTIONS TO SOLOMON

¹ As the time approached for David to die, he ordered his son Solomon, ² "As for me, I am going the way of all of the earth. Be strong and be a man, ³ and keep your obligation to the LORD your God to walk in his ways and to keep his statutes, commands, ordinances, and decrees. This is written in the law of Moses, so that you will have success in everything you do and wherever you turn, ⁴ and so that the LORD will fulfill his promise that he made to me: 'If your sons take care to walk faithfully before me with all their heart and all their soul, you will never fail to have a man on the throne of Israel.'"

. . .

¹⁰ Then David rested with his ancestors and was buried in the city of David. ¹¹ The length of time David reigned over Israel was forty years: he reigned seven years in Hebron and thirty-three years in Jerusalem. ¹² Solomon sat on the throne of his father David, and his kingship was firmly established.

1 KINGS 3:1-15

THE LORD APPEARS TO SOLOMON

¹ Solomon made an alliance with Pharaoh king of Egypt by marrying Pharaoh's daughter. Solomon brought her to the city of David until he finished building his palace, the LORD's temple, and the wall surrounding Jerusalem. ² However, the people were sacrificing on the high places, because until that time a temple for the LORD's name had not been built. ³ Solomon loved the LORD by walking in the statutes of his father David, but he also sacrificed and burned incense on the high places.

⁴ The king went to Gibeon to sacrifice there because it was the most famous high place. He offered a thousand burnt offerings on that altar. ⁵ At Gibeon the LORD appeared to Solomon in a dream at night. God said, "Ask. What should I give you?"

⁶ And Solomon replied, "You have shown great and faithful love to your servant, my father David, because he walked before you in faithfulness, righteousness, and integrity. You have continued this great and faithful love for him by giving him a son to sit on his throne, as it is today.

[7] "LORD my God, you have now made your servant king in my father David's place. Yet I am just a youth with no experience in leadership. [8] Your servant is among your people you have chosen, a people too many to be numbered or counted. [9] So give your servant a receptive heart to judge your people and to discern between good and evil. For who is able to judge this great people of yours?"

[10] Now it pleased the Lord that Solomon had requested this. [11] So God said to him, "Because you have requested this and did not ask for long life or riches for yourself, or the death of your enemies, but you asked discernment for yourself to administer justice, [12] I will therefore do what you have asked. I will give you a wise and understanding heart, so that there has never been anyone like you before and never will be again. [13] In addition, I will give you what you did not ask for: both riches and honor, so that no king will be your equal during your entire life. [14] If you walk in my ways and keep my statutes and commands just as your father David did, I will give you a long life."

[15] Then Solomon woke up and realized it had been a dream. He went to Jerusalem, stood before the ark of the Lord's covenant, and offered burnt offerings and fellowship offerings. Then he held a feast for all his servants.

1 KINGS 4:29-34

SOLOMON'S WISDOM AND LITERARY GIFTS

[29] God gave Solomon wisdom, very great insight, and understanding as vast as the sand on the seashore. [30] Solomon's wisdom was greater than the wisdom of all the people of the East, greater than all the wisdom of Egypt. [31] He was wiser than anyone—wiser than Ethan the Ezrahite, and Heman, Calcol, and Darda, sons of Mahol. His reputation extended to all the surrounding nations.

[32] Solomon spoke 3,000 proverbs, and his songs numbered 1,005. [33] He spoke about trees, from the cedar in Lebanon to the hyssop growing out of the wall. He also spoke about animals, birds, reptiles, and fish. [34] Emissaries of all peoples, sent by every king on earth who had heard of his wisdom, came to listen to Solomon's wisdom.

1 KINGS 6:37-38

[37] The foundation of the LORD's temple was laid in Solomon's fourth year in the month of Ziv. [38] In his eleventh year in the month of Bul, which is the eighth month, the temple was completed in every detail and according to every specification. So he built it in seven years.

1 KINGS 8:1-13

SOLOMON'S DEDICATION OF THE TEMPLE

[1] At that time Solomon assembled the elders of Israel, all the tribal heads and the ancestral leaders of the Israelites before him at Jerusalem in order to bring the ark of the LORD's covenant from the city of David, that is Zion. [2] So all the men of Israel were assembled in the presence of King Solomon in the month of Ethanim, which is the seventh month, at the festival.

[3] All the elders of Israel came, and the priests picked up the ark. [4] The priests and the Levites brought the ark of the LORD, the tent of meeting, and the holy utensils that were in the tent. [5] King Solomon and the entire congregation of Israel, who had gathered around him and were with him in front of the ark, were sacrificing

sheep, goats, and cattle that could not be counted or numbered, because there were so many. ⁶ The priests brought the ark of the Lord's covenant to its place, into the inner sanctuary of the temple, to the most holy place beneath the wings of the cherubim. ⁷ For the cherubim were spreading their wings over the place of the ark, so that the cherubim covered the ark and its poles from above. ⁸ The poles were so long that their ends were seen from the holy place in front of the inner sanctuary, but they were not seen from outside the sanctuary; they are still there today. ⁹ Nothing was in the ark except the two stone tablets that Moses had put there at Horeb, where the Lord made a covenant with the Israelites when they came out of the land of Egypt.

¹⁰ When the priests came out of the holy place, the cloud filled the Lord's temple, ¹¹ and because of the cloud, the priests were not able to continue ministering, for the glory of the Lord filled the temple.

¹² Then Solomon said:

The Lord said that he would dwell in total darkness.
¹³ I have indeed built an exalted temple for you,
a place for your dwelling forever.

1 KINGS 9:1-5

THE LORD'S RESPONSE

¹ When Solomon finished building the temple of the Lord, the royal palace, and all that Solomon desired to do, ² the Lord appeared to Solomon a second time just as he had appeared to him at Gibeon. ³ The Lord said to him:

I have heard your prayer and petition you have made before me. I have consecrated this temple you have built, to put my name there forever; my eyes and my heart will be there at all times.

⁴ As for you, if you walk before me as your father David walked, with a heart of integrity and in what is right, doing everything I have commanded you, and if you keep my statutes and ordinances, ⁵ I will establish your royal throne over Israel forever, as I promised your father David: You will never fail to have a man on the throne of Israel.

1 KINGS 11:1-13

SOLOMON'S UNFAITHFULNESS TO GOD

¹ King Solomon loved many foreign women in addition to Pharaoh's daughter: Moabite, Ammonite, Edomite, Sidonian, and Hittite women ² from the nations about which the LORD had told the Israelites, "You must not intermarry with them, and they must not intermarry with you, because they will turn your heart away to follow their gods." To these women Solomon was deeply attached in love. ³ He had seven hundred wives who were princesses and three hundred who were concubines, and they turned his heart away.

⁴ When Solomon was old, his wives turned his heart away to follow other gods. He was not wholeheartedly devoted to the LORD his God, as his father David had been. ⁵ Solomon followed Ashtoreth, the goddess of the Sidonians, and Milcom, the abhorrent idol of the Ammonites. ⁶ Solomon did what was evil in the LORD's sight, and unlike his father David, he did not remain loyal to the LORD.

⁷ At that time, Solomon built a high place for Chemosh, the abhorrent idol of Moab, and for Milcom, the abhorrent idol of the Ammonites, on the hill across from Jerusalem. ⁸ He did the same for all his foreign wives, who were burning incense and offering sacrifices to their gods.

⁹ The LORD was angry with Solomon, because his heart had turned away from the LORD, the God of Israel, who had appeared to him twice. ¹⁰ He had commanded him about this, so that he would not follow other gods, but Solomon did not do what the LORD had commanded.

¹¹ Then the LORD said to Solomon, "Since you have done this and did not keep my covenant and my statutes, which I commanded you, I will tear the kingdom away from you and give it to your servant. ¹² However, I will not do it during your lifetime for the sake of your father David; I will tear it out of your son's hand. ¹³ Yet I will not tear the entire kingdom away from him. I will give one tribe to your son for the sake of my servant David and for the sake of Jerusalem that I chose."

RESPOND

1. WHERE DO I SEE GOD AT WORK IN SOLOMON'S STORY?

2. HOW DO I CONNECT TO SOLOMON'S EXPERIENCES? IN WHAT WAYS DO HIS EXPERIENCES FEEL FOREIGN TO ME?

3. AFTER READING SOLOMON'S STORY, WHAT DO I WANT TO CONTINUE TO MEDITATE ON?

GRACE DAY

TAKE THIS DAY TO CATCH UP ON
YOUR READING, PRAY, AND REST IN
THE PRESENCE OF THE LORD.

THEREFORE, BROTHERS AND
SISTERS, IN VIEW OF THE MERCIES
OF GOD, I URGE YOU TO PRESENT
YOUR BODIES AS A LIVING SACRIFICE,
HOLY AND PLEASING TO GOD; THIS IS
YOUR TRUE WORSHIP.

ROMANS 12:1

WEEKLY

DAY

SCRIPTURE IS GOD BREATHED AND TRUE.
WHEN WE MEMORIZE IT, WE CARRY THE GOOD
NEWS OF JESUS WITH US WHEREVER WE GO.

FOR THIS PLAN, WE ARE MEMORIZING OUR KEY
PASSAGE, PSALM 8:3–4. WE WILL CONTINUE
WITH THE FIFTH LINE.

SEE TIPS FOR MEMORIZING SCRIPTURE ON PAGE 236.

TRUTH

PSALM 8:3-4

WHEN I OBSERVE YOUR HEAVENS,
THE WORK OF YOUR FINGERS,
THE MOON AND THE STARS,
WHICH YOU SET IN PLACE,
<u>WHAT IS A HUMAN BEING THAT YOU REMEMBER HIM,</u>
A SON OF MAN THAT YOU LOOK AFTER HIM?

ELIJAH

THE PROPHET GOD USED TO TURN THE HEARTS OF HIS PEOPLE

ELIJAH APPROACHED ALL THE PEOPLE AND SAID, "HOW LONG WILL YOU WAVER BETWEEN TWO OPINIONS? IF THE LORD IS GOD, FOLLOW HIM. BUT IF BAAL, FOLLOW HIM." BUT THE PEOPLE DIDN'T ANSWER HIM A WORD. —1 KINGS 18:21

ISRAEL'S KING AHAB

²⁹ Ahab son of Omri became king over Israel in the thirty-eighth year of Judah's King Asa; Ahab son of Omri reigned over Israel in Samaria twenty-two years. ³⁰ But Ahab son of Omri did what was evil in the Lord's sight more than all who were before him. ³¹ Then, as if following the sin of Jeroboam son of Nebat were not enough, he married Jezebel, the daughter of Ethbaal king of the Sidonians, and then proceeded to serve Baal and bow in worship to him. ³² He set up an altar for Baal in the temple of Baal that he had built in Samaria. ³³ Ahab also made an Asherah pole. Ahab did more to anger the Lord God of Israel than all the kings of Israel who were before him.

1 KINGS 17:1-7

ELIJAH ANNOUNCES FAMINE

¹ Now Elijah the Tishbite, from the Gilead settlers, said to Ahab, "As the Lord God of Israel lives, in whose presence I stand, there will be no dew or rain during these years except by my command!"

² Then the word of the Lord came to him: ³ "Leave here, turn eastward, and hide at the Wadi Cherith where it enters the Jordan. ⁴ You are to drink from the wadi. I have commanded the ravens to provide for you there."

⁵ So he proceeded to do what the Lord commanded. Elijah left and lived at the Wadi Cherith where it enters the Jordan. ⁶ The ravens kept bringing him bread and meat in the morning and in the evening, and he would drink from the wadi. ⁷ After a while, the wadi dried up because there had been no rain in the land.

1 KINGS 18

ELIJAH'S MESSAGE TO AHAB

¹ After a long time, the word of the Lord came to Elijah in the third year: "Go and present yourself to Ahab. I will send rain on the surface of the land." ² So Elijah went to present himself to Ahab.

The famine was severe in Samaria. ³ Ahab called for Obadiah, who was in charge of the palace. Obadiah was a man who greatly feared the Lord ⁴ and took a hundred prophets and hid them, fifty men to a cave, and provided them with food and water when Jezebel slaughtered the Lord's prophets. ⁵ Ahab said to Obadiah, "Go throughout the land to every spring and to every wadi. Perhaps we'll find grass so we can keep the horses and mules alive and not have to destroy any cattle." ⁶ They divided the land between them in order to cover it. Ahab went one way by himself, and Obadiah went the other way by himself.

⁷ While Obadiah was walking along the road, Elijah suddenly met him. When Obadiah recognized him, he fell facedown and said, "Is it you, my lord Elijah?"

⁸ "It is I," he replied. "Go tell your lord, 'Elijah is here!'"

⁹ But Obadiah said, "What sin have I committed, that you are handing your servant over to Ahab to put me to death? ¹⁰ As the Lord your God lives, there is no nation or kingdom where my lord has not sent someone to search for you. When they said, 'He is not here,' he made that kingdom or nation swear they had not found you.

¹¹ "Now you say, 'Go tell your lord, "Elijah is here!"' ¹² But when I leave you, the Spirit of the Lord may carry you off to some place I don't know. Then when I go report to Ahab and he doesn't find you, he will kill me. But I, your servant, have feared the Lord from my youth. ¹³ Wasn't it reported to my lord what I did when Jezebel slaughtered the Lord's prophets? I hid a hundred of the prophets of the Lord, fifty men to a cave, and I provided them with food and water. ¹⁴ Now you say, 'Go tell your lord, "Elijah is here!"' He will kill me!"

¹⁵ Then Elijah said, "As the Lord of Armies lives, in whose presence I stand, today I will present myself to Ahab."

¹⁶ Obadiah went to meet Ahab and told him. Then Ahab went to meet Elijah. ¹⁷ When Ahab saw Elijah, Ahab said to him, "Is that you, the one ruining Israel?"

¹⁸ He replied, "I have not ruined Israel, but you and your father's family have, because you have abandoned the Lord's commands and followed the Baals. ¹⁹ Now summon all Israel to meet me at Mount Carmel, along with the 450 prophets of Baal and the 400 prophets of Asherah who eat at Jezebel's table."

[20] So Ahab summoned all the Israelites and gathered the prophets at Mount Carmel. [21] Then Elijah approached all the people and said, "How long will you waver between two opinions? If the LORD is God, follow him. But if Baal, follow him." But the people didn't answer him a word.

[22] Then Elijah said to the people, "I am the only remaining prophet of the LORD, but Baal's prophets are 450 men. [23] Let two bulls be given to us. They are to choose one bull for themselves, cut it in pieces, and place it on the wood but not light the fire. I will prepare the other bull and place it on the wood but not light the fire. [24] Then you call on the name of your god, and I will call on the name of the LORD. The God who answers with fire, he is God."

All the people answered, "That's fine."

[25] Then Elijah said to the prophets of Baal, "Since you are so numerous, choose for yourselves one bull and prepare it first. Then call on the name of your god but don't light the fire."

[26] So they took the bull that he gave them, prepared it, and called on the name of Baal from morning until noon, saying, "Baal, answer us!" But there was no sound; no one answered. Then they danced around the altar they had made.

[27] At noon Elijah mocked them. He said, "Shout loudly, for he's a god! Maybe he's thinking it over; maybe he has wandered away; or maybe he's on the road. Perhaps he's sleeping and will wake up!" [28] They shouted loudly, and cut themselves with knives and spears, according to their custom, until blood gushed over them. [29] All afternoon they kept on raving until the offering of the evening sacrifice, but there was no sound; no one answered, no one paid attention.

[30] Then Elijah said to all the people, "Come near me." So all the people approached him. Then he repaired the LORD's altar that had been torn down: [31] Elijah took twelve stones—according to the number of the tribes of the sons of Jacob, to whom the word of the LORD had come, saying, "Israel will be your name"— [32] and he built an altar with the stones in the name of the LORD. Then he made a trench around the altar large enough to hold about four gallons. [33] Next, he arranged the wood,

cut up the bull, and placed it on the wood. He said, "Fill four water pots with water and pour it on the offering to be burned and on the wood." ³⁴ Then he said, "A second time!" and they did it a second time. And then he said, "A third time!" and they did it a third time. ³⁵ So the water ran all around the altar; he even filled the trench with water.

³⁶ At the time for offering the evening sacrifice, the prophet Elijah approached the altar and said, "LORD, the God of Abraham, Isaac, and Israel, today let it be known that you are God in Israel and I am your servant, and that at your word I have done all these things. ³⁷ Answer me, LORD! Answer me so that this people will know that you, the LORD, are God and that you have turned their hearts back."

³⁸ Then the LORD's fire fell and consumed the burnt offering, the wood, the stones, and the dust, and it licked up the water that was in the trench. ³⁹ When all the people saw it, they fell facedown and said, "The LORD, he is God! The LORD, he is God!"

⁴⁰ Then Elijah ordered them, "Seize the prophets of Baal! Do not let even one of them escape." So they seized them, and Elijah brought them down to the Wadi Kishon and slaughtered them there. ⁴¹ Elijah said to Ahab, "Go up, eat and drink, for there is the sound of a rainstorm."

⁴² So Ahab went to eat and drink, but Elijah went up to the summit of Carmel. He bent down on the ground and put his face between his knees. ⁴³ Then he said to his servant, "Go up and look toward the sea."

So he went up, looked, and said, "There's nothing."

Seven times Elijah said, "Go back."

⁴⁴ On the seventh time, he reported, "There's a cloud as small as a man's hand coming up from the sea."

Then Elijah said, "Go and tell Ahab, 'Get your chariot ready and go down so the rain doesn't stop you.'"

⁴⁵ In a little while, the sky grew dark with clouds and wind, and there was a downpour. So Ahab got in his chariot and went to Jezreel. ⁴⁶ The power of the LORD was on Elijah, and he tucked his mantle under his belt and ran ahead of Ahab to the entrance of Jezreel.

RESPOND

01 WHERE DO I SEE GOD AT WORK IN
    ELIJAH'S STORY?

02 HOW DO I CONNECT TO ELIJAH'S
    EXPERIENCES? IN WHAT WAYS DO HIS
    EXPERIENCES FEEL FOREIGN TO ME?

_____   _____
_____   _____
_____   _____
_____   _____
_____   _____
_____   _____
_____   _____
_____   _____
_____   _____
_____   _____

03 AFTER READING ELIJAHS STORY, WHAT DO I WANT TO CONTINUE TO MEDITATE ON?

_____
_____
_____
_____
_____
_____
_____
_____
_____

HOSEA & GOMER

DAY 37　　　　　　　　　　　　　　　　　　　　　　　WEEK 6

HOSEA 1:2-11

HOSEA'S MARRIAGE AND CHILDREN

² When the LORD first spoke to Hosea, he said this to him:

> Go and marry a woman of promiscuity,
> and have children of promiscuity,
> for the land is committing blatant acts
>   of promiscuity
> by abandoning the LORD.

³ So he went and married Gomer daughter of Diblaim, and she conceived and bore him a son. ⁴ Then the LORD said to him:

> Name him Jezreel, for in a little while
> I will bring the bloodshed of Jezreel
> on the house of Jehu
> and put an end to the kingdom of the house
>   of Israel.
> ⁵ On that day I will break the bow of Israel
> in Jezreel Valley.

⁶ She conceived again and gave birth to a daughter, and the LORD said to him:

> Name her Lo-ruhamah,
> for I will no longer have compassion
> on the house of Israel.
> I will certainly take them away.
> ⁷ But I will have compassion on the house
>   of Judah,
> and I will deliver them by the LORD their God.
> I will not deliver them by bow, sword, or war,
> or by horses and cavalry.

⁸ After Gomer had weaned Lo-ruhamah, she conceived and gave birth to a son. ⁹ Then the LORD said:

> Name him Lo-ammi,
> for you are not my people,
> and I will not be your God.
> ¹⁰ Yet the number of the Israelites
> will be like the sand of the sea,
> which cannot be measured or counted.
> And in the place where they were told:
> You are not my people,
> they will be called: Sons of the living God.

¹¹ And the Judeans and the Israelites
will be gathered together.
They will appoint for themselves a single ruler
and go up from the land.
For the day of Jezreel will be great.

HOSEA 2:1, 5–23

¹ Call your brothers: My People
and your sisters: Compassion.

...

⁵ Yes, their mother is promiscuous;
she conceived them and acted shamefully.
For she thought, "I will follow my lovers,
the men who give me my food and water,
my wool and flax, my oil and drink."
⁶ Therefore, this is what I will do:
I will block her way with thorns;
I will enclose her with a wall,
so that she cannot find her paths.
⁷ She will pursue her lovers but not catch them;
she will look for them but not find them.
Then she will think,
"I will go back to my former husband,
for then it was better for me than now."
⁸ She does not recognize
that it is I who gave her the grain,
the new wine, and the fresh oil.
I lavished silver and gold on her,
which they used for Baal.
⁹ Therefore, I will take back my grain in its time
and my new wine in its season;
I will take away my wool and linen,
which were to cover her nakedness.
¹⁰ Now I will expose her shame
in the sight of her lovers,
and no one will rescue her from my power.
¹¹ I will put an end to all her celebrations:
her feasts, New Moons, and Sabbaths—
all her festivals.

¹² I will devastate her vines and fig trees.
She thinks that these are her wages
that her lovers have given her.
I will turn them into a thicket,
and the wild animals will eat them.
¹³ And I will punish her for the days of
the Baals,
to which she burned incense.
She put on her rings and her jewelry
and followed her lovers,
but she forgot me.

This is the LORD's declaration.

ISRAEL'S ADULTERY FORGIVEN

¹⁴ Therefore, I am going to persuade her,
lead her to the wilderness,
and speak tenderly to her.
¹⁵ There I will give her vineyards back to her
and make the Valley of Achor
into a gateway of hope.
There she will respond as she did
in the days of her youth,
as in the day she came out of the land
of Egypt.
¹⁶ In that day—
this is the LORD's declaration—
you will call me "my husband"
and no longer call me "my Baal."
¹⁷ For I will remove the names of the Baals
from her mouth;
they will no longer be remembered by
their names.
¹⁸ On that day I will make a covenant
for them
with the wild animals, the birds of the sky,
and the creatures that crawl on the ground.
I will shatter bow, sword,
and weapons of war in the land
and will enable the people to rest securely.
¹⁹ I will take you to be my wife forever.

I will take you to be my wife
in righteousness,
justice, love, and compassion.
²⁰ I will take you to be my wife in faithfulness,
and you will know the LORD.
²¹ On that day I will respond—
this is the LORD's declaration.
I will respond to the sky,
and it will respond to the earth.
²² The earth will respond to the grain,
the new wine, and the fresh oil,
and they will respond to Jezreel.
²³ I will sow her in the land for myself,
and I will have compassion
on Lo-ruhamah;
I will say to Lo-ammi:
You are my people,
and he will say, "You are my God."

HOSEA 3:1-5

WAITING FOR RESTORATION

¹ Then the LORD said to me, "Go again; show love to a woman who is loved by another man and is an adulteress, just as the LORD loves the Israelites though they turn to other gods and love raisin cakes."

² So I bought her for fifteen shekels of silver and nine bushels of barley. ³ I said to her, "You are to live with me many days. You must not be promiscuous or belong to any man, and I will act the same way toward you."

⁴ For the Israelites must live many days without king or prince, without sacrifice or sacred pillar, and without ephod or household idols. ⁵ Afterward, the people of Israel will return and seek the LORD their God and David their king. They will come with awe to the LORD and to his goodness in the last days.

RESPOND

DATE   /   /

01 WHERE DO I SEE GOD AT WORK IN
    HOSEA AND GOMER'S STORY?

_____

_____

_____

_____

_____

_____

_____

_____

_____

_____

02 HOW DO I CONNECT TO HOSEA AND
    GOMER'S EXPERIENCES? IN WHAT
    WAYS DO THEIR EXPERIENCES FEEL
    FOREIGN TO ME?

_____

_____

_____

_____

_____

_____

_____

_____

_____

03 AFTER READING HOSEA AND GOMER'S STORY, WHAT DO I WANT TO CONTINUE TO
    MEDITATE ON?

_____

_____

_____

_____

_____

_____

_____

_____

_____

JOSIAH

THE KING WHO RESTORED
THE BOOK OF THE LAW

JUDAH'S KING JOSIAH

¹ Josiah was eight years old when he became king, and he reigned thirty-one years in Jerusalem. His mother's name was Jedidah the daughter of Adaiah; she was from Bozkath. ² He did what was right in the LORD's sight and walked in all the ways of his ancestor David; he did not turn to the right or the left.

JOSIAH REPAIRS THE TEMPLE

³ In the eighteenth year of King Josiah, the king sent the court secretary Shaphan son of Azaliah, son of Meshullam, to the LORD's temple, saying, ⁴ "Go up to the high priest Hilkiah so that he may total up the silver brought into the LORD's temple—the silver the doorkeepers have collected from the people. ⁵ It is to be given to those doing the work—those who oversee the LORD's temple. They in turn are to give it to the workmen in the LORD's temple to repair the damage. ⁶ They are to give it to the carpenters, builders, and masons to buy timber and quarried stone to repair the temple. ⁷ But no accounting is to be required from them for the silver given to them since they work with integrity."

THE BOOK OF THE LAW FOUND

⁸ The high priest Hilkiah told the court secretary Shaphan, "I have found the book of the law in the LORD's temple," and he gave the book to Shaphan, who read it.

⁹ Then the court secretary Shaphan went to the king and reported, "Your servants have emptied out the silver that was found in the temple and have given it to those doing the work—those who oversee the LORD's temple." ¹⁰ Then the court secretary Shaphan told the king, "The priest Hilkiah has given me a book," and Shaphan read it in the presence of the king.

¹¹ When the king heard the words of the book of the law, he tore his clothes. ¹² Then he commanded the priest Hilkiah, Ahikam son of Shaphan, Achbor son of Micaiah, the court secretary Shaphan, and the king's servant Asaiah, ¹³ "Go and inquire of the LORD for me, for the people, and for all Judah about the words in this book that has been found. For great is the LORD's wrath that is kindled against us because our ancestors have not obeyed the words of this book in order to do everything written about us."

[14] So the priest Hilkiah, Ahikam, Achbor, Shaphan, and Asaiah went to the prophetess Huldah, wife of Shallum son of Tikvah, son of Harhas, keeper of the wardrobe. She lived in Jerusalem in the Second District. They spoke with her.

[15] She said to them, "This is what the LORD God of Israel says: Say to the man who sent you to me, [16] 'This is what the LORD says: I am about to bring disaster on this place and on its inhabitants, fulfilling all the words of the book that the king of Judah has read, [17] because they have abandoned me and burned incense to other gods in order to anger me with all the work of their hands. My wrath will be kindled against this place, and it will not be quenched.' [18] Say this to the king of Judah who sent you to inquire of the LORD: 'This is what the LORD God of Israel says: As for the words that you heard, [19] because your heart was tender and you humbled yourself before the LORD when you heard what I spoke against this place and against its inhabitants, that they would become a desolation and a curse, and because you have torn your clothes and wept before me, I myself have heard'—this is the LORD's declaration. [20] 'Therefore, I will indeed gather you to your ancestors, and you will be gathered to your grave in peace. Your eyes will not see all the disaster that I am bringing on this place.'"

Then they reported to the king.

2 KINGS 23:1-15, 21-27

COVENANT RENEWAL

[1] So the king sent messengers, and they gathered all the elders of Judah and Jerusalem to him. [2] Then the king went to the LORD's temple with all the men of Judah and all the inhabitants of Jerusalem, as well as the priests and the prophets—all the people from the youngest to the oldest. He read in their hearing all the words of the book of the covenant that had been found in the LORD's temple. [3] Next, the king stood by the pillar and made a covenant in the LORD's presence to follow the LORD and to keep his commands, his decrees, and his statutes with all his heart and with all his soul in order to carry out the words of this covenant that were written in this book; all the people agreed to the covenant.

⁴ Then the king commanded the high priest Hilkiah and the priests of the second rank and the doorkeepers to bring out of the Lᴏʀᴅ's sanctuary all the articles made for Baal, Asherah, and all the stars in the sky. He burned them outside Jerusalem in the fields of the Kidron and carried their ashes to Bethel. ⁵ Then he did away with the idolatrous priests the kings of Judah had appointed to burn incense at the high places in the cities of Judah and in the areas surrounding Jerusalem. They had burned incense to Baal, and to the sun, moon, constellations, and all the stars in the sky. ⁶ He brought out the Asherah pole from the Lᴏʀᴅ's temple to the Kidron Valley outside Jerusalem. He burned it at the Kidron Valley, beat it to dust, and threw its dust on the graves of the common people. ⁷ He also tore down the houses of the male cult prostitutes that were in the Lᴏʀᴅ's temple, in which the women were weaving tapestries for Asherah.

⁸ Then Josiah brought all the priests from the cities of Judah, and he defiled the high places from Geba to Beer-sheba, where the priests had burned incense. He tore down the high places of the city gates at the entrance of the gate of Joshua the governor of the city (on the left at the city gate). ⁹ The priests of the high places, however, did not come up to the altar of the Lᴏʀᴅ in Jerusalem; instead, they ate unleavened bread with their fellow priests.

¹⁰ He defiled Topheth, which is in Ben Hinnom Valley, so that no one could sacrifice his son or daughter in the fire to Molech. ¹¹ He did away with the horses that the kings of Judah had dedicated to the sun. They had been at the entrance of the Lᴏʀᴅ's temple in the precincts by the chamber of Nathan-melech, the eunuch. He also burned the chariots of the sun.

¹² The king tore down the altars that the kings of Judah had made on the roof of Ahaz's upper chamber. He also tore down the altars that Manasseh had made in the two courtyards of the Lᴏʀᴅ's temple. Then he smashed them there and threw their dust into the Kidron Valley. ¹³ The king also defiled the high places that were across from Jerusalem, to the south of the Mount of Destruction, which King Solomon of Israel had built for Ashtoreth, the abhorrent idol of the Sidonians; for Chemosh, the abhorrent idol of Moab; and for Milcom, the detestable idol of the Ammonites. ¹⁴ He broke the sacred pillars into pieces, cut down the Asherah poles, then filled their places with human bones.

[15] He even tore down the altar at Bethel and the high place that had been made by Jeroboam son of Nebat, who caused Israel to sin. He burned the high place, crushed it to dust, and burned the Asherah.

...

PASSOVER OBSERVED

[21] The king commanded all the people, "Observe the Passover of the LORD your God as written in the book of the covenant." [22] No such Passover had ever been observed from the time of the judges who judged Israel through the entire time of the kings of Israel and Judah. [23] But in the eighteenth year of King Josiah, the LORD's Passover was observed in Jerusalem.

FURTHER ZEAL FOR THE LORD

[24] In addition,

JOSIAH ERADICATED THE MEDIUMS, THE SPIRITISTS, HOUSEHOLD IDOLS, IMAGES, AND ALL THE ABHORRENT THINGS THAT WERE SEEN IN THE LAND OF JUDAH AND IN JERUSALEM.

He did this in order to carry out the words of the law that were written in the book that the priest Hilkiah found in the LORD's temple. [25] Before him there was no king like him who turned to the LORD with all his heart and with all his soul and with all his strength according to all the law of Moses, and no one like him arose after him.

[26] In spite of all that, the LORD did not turn from the fury of his intense burning anger, which burned against Judah because of all the affronts with which Manasseh had angered him. [27] For the LORD had said, "I will also remove Judah from my presence just as I have removed Israel. I will reject this city Jerusalem, that I have chosen, and the temple about which I said, 'My name will be there.'"

RESPOND

01 WHERE DO I SEE GOD AT WORK IN
JOSIAH'S STORY?

02 HOW DO I CONNECT TO JOSIAH'S
EXPERIENCES? IN WHAT WAYS DO HIS
EXPERIENCES FEEL FOREIGN TO ME?

_____   _____
_____   _____
_____   _____
_____   _____
_____   _____
_____   _____
_____   _____
_____   _____
_____   _____

03 AFTER READING JOSIAH'S STORY, WHAT DO I WANT TO CONTINUE TO MEDITATE ON?

_____
_____
_____
_____
_____
_____
_____
_____
_____

EZEKIEL

DAY 39  WEEK 6

EZEKIEL 2

MISSION TO REBELLIOUS ISRAEL

¹ He said to me, "Son of man, stand up on your feet and I will speak with you." ² As he spoke to me, the Spirit entered me and set me on my feet, and I listened to the one who was speaking to me. ³ He said to me, "Son of man, I am sending you to the Israelites, to the rebellious pagans who have rebelled against me. The Israelites and their ancestors have transgressed against me to this day. ⁴ The descendants are obstinate and hardhearted. I am sending you to them, and you must say to them, 'This is what the Lord God says.' ⁵ Whether they listen or refuse to listen—for they are a rebellious house—they will know that a prophet has been among them.

⁶ "But you, son of man, do not be afraid of them and do not be afraid of their words, even though briers and thorns are beside you and you live among scorpions. Don't be afraid of their words or discouraged by the look on their faces, for they are a rebellious house. ⁷ Speak my words to them whether they listen or refuse to listen, for they are rebellious.

⁸ "And you, son of man, listen to what I tell you: Do not be rebellious like that rebellious house.

Open your mouth and eat what I am giving you." ⁹ So I looked and saw a hand reaching out to me, and there was a written scroll in it. ¹⁰ When he unrolled it before me, it was written on the front and back; words of lamentation, mourning, and woe were written on it.

EZEKIEL 3:1-15

¹ He said to me, "Son of man, eat what you find here. Eat this scroll, then go and speak to the house of Israel." ² So I opened my mouth, and he fed me the scroll. ³ "Son of man," he said to me, "feed your stomach and fill your belly with this scroll I am giving you." So I ate it, and it was as sweet as honey in my mouth.

⁴ Then he said to me, "Son of man, go to the house of Israel and speak my words to them. ⁵ For you are not being sent to a people of unintelligible speech or a difficult language but to the house of Israel— ⁶ not to the many peoples of unintelligible speech or a difficult language, whose words you cannot understand. No doubt, if I sent you to them, they would listen to you. ⁷ But the house of Israel will not want to listen to you because they do not

want to listen to me. For the whole house of Israel is hardheaded and hardhearted. ⁸ Look, I have made your face as hard as their faces and your forehead as hard as their foreheads. ⁹ I have made your forehead like a diamond, harder than flint. Don't be afraid of them or discouraged by the look on their faces, though they are a rebellious house."

¹⁰ Next he said to me, "Son of man, listen carefully to all my words that I speak to you and take them to heart. ¹¹ Go to your people, the exiles, and speak to them. Tell them, 'This is what the Lord GOD says,' whether they listen or refuse to listen."

¹² The Spirit then lifted me up, and I heard a loud rumbling sound behind me—bless the glory of the LORD in his place!— ¹³ with the sound of the living creatures' wings brushing against each other and the sound of the wheels beside them, a loud rumbling sound. ¹⁴ The Spirit lifted me up and took me away. I left in bitterness and in an angry spirit, and the LORD's hand was on me powerfully. ¹⁵ I came to the exiles at Tel-abib, who were living by the Chebar Canal, and I sat there among them stunned for seven days.

EZEKIEL 12:1-20

EZEKIEL DRAMATIZES THE EXILE

¹ The word of the LORD came to me: ² "Son of man, you are living among a rebellious house. They have eyes to see but do not see, and ears to hear but do not hear, for they are a rebellious house.

³ "Now you, son of man, get your bags ready for exile and go into exile in their sight during the day. You will go into exile from your place to another place while they watch; perhaps they will understand, though they are a rebellious house. ⁴ During the day, bring out your bags like an exile's bags while they look on. Then in the evening go out in their sight like those going into exile. ⁵ As they watch, dig through the wall and take the bags out through it. ⁶ And while they look on, lift the bags to your shoulder and take them out in the dark; cover your face so that you cannot see the land.

FOR I HAVE MADE YOU A SIGN TO THE HOUSE OF ISRAEL."

⁷ So I did just as I was commanded. In the daytime I brought out my bags like an exile's bags. In the evening I dug through the wall by hand; I took them out in the dark, carrying them on my shoulder in their sight.

⁸ In the morning the word of the LORD came to me: ⁹ "Son of man, hasn't the house of Israel, that rebellious house, asked you, 'What are you doing?' ¹⁰ Say to them, 'This is what the Lord GOD says: This pronouncement concerns the prince in Jerusalem and the whole house of Israel living there.' ¹¹ You are to say, 'I am a sign for you. Just as I have done, it will be done to them; they will go into exile, into captivity.' ¹² The prince who is among them will lift his bags to his shoulder in the dark and go out. They will dig through the wall to bring him out through it. He will cover his face so he cannot see the land with his eyes. ¹³ But I will spread my net over him, and he will be caught in my snare. I will bring him to Babylon, the land of the Chaldeans, yet he will not see it, and he will die there. ¹⁴ I will also scatter all the attendants who surround him and all his troops to every direction of the wind, and I will draw a sword to chase after them. ¹⁵ They will know that I am the LORD when I disperse them among the nations and scatter them among the countries. ¹⁶ But I will spare a few of them from the sword, famine, and plague, so that among the nations where they go they can tell about all their detestable practices. Then they will know that I am the LORD."

EZEKIEL DRAMATIZES ISRAEL'S ANXIETY

¹⁷ The word of the LORD came to me: ¹⁸ "Son of man, eat your bread with trembling and drink your water with anxious shaking. ¹⁹ Then say to the people of the land, 'This is what the Lord GOD says about the residents of Jerusalem in the land of Israel: They will eat their bread with anxiety and drink their water in dread, for their land will be stripped of everything in it because of the violence of all who live there. ²⁰ The inhabited cities will be destroyed, and the land will become dreadful. Then you will know that I am the LORD.'"

RESPOND

01 WHERE DO I SEE GOD AT WORK IN EZEKIEL'S STORY?

_____
_____
_____
_____
_____
_____
_____
_____
_____
_____
_____

02 HOW DO I CONNECT TO EZEKIEL'S EXPERIENCES? IN WHAT WAYS DO HIS EXPERIENCES FEEL FOREIGN TO ME?

_____
_____
_____
_____
_____
_____
_____
_____
_____
_____

03 AFTER READING EZEKIEL'S STORY, WHAT DO I WANT TO CONTINUE TO MEDITATE ON?

_____
_____
_____
_____
_____
_____
_____
_____
_____

JEREMIAH

THE PROPHET WHO WAS FILLED WITH GOD'S WORDS

JEREMIAH 1:1–10

¹ The words of Jeremiah, the son of Hilkiah, one of the priests living in Anathoth in the territory of Benjamin. ² The word of the Lord came to him in the thirteenth year of the reign of Josiah son of Amon, king of Judah. ³ It also came throughout the days of Jehoiakim son of Josiah, king of Judah, until the fifth month of the eleventh year of Zedekiah son of Josiah, king of Judah, when the people of Jerusalem went into exile.

THE CALL OF JEREMIAH

⁴ The word of the Lord came to me:

⁵ I chose you before I formed you in the womb;
I set you apart before you were born.
I appointed you a prophet to the nations.

⁶ But I protested, "Oh no, Lord God! Look, I don't know how to speak since I am only a youth."

⁷ Then the Lord said to me:

Do not say, "I am only a youth,"
for you will go to everyone I send you to
and speak whatever I tell you.

⁸ Do not be afraid of anyone,

for I will be with you to rescue you.

   This is the LORD's declaration.

⁹ Then the LORD reached out his hand, touched my mouth, and told me:

I have now filled your mouth with my words.

¹⁰ See, I have appointed you today

over nations and kingdoms

to uproot and tear down,

to destroy and demolish,

to build and plant.

JEREMIAH 29:1, 4–19

JEREMIAH'S LETTER TO THE EXILES

¹ This is the text of the letter that the prophet Jeremiah sent from Jerusalem to the remaining exiled elders, the priests, the prophets, and all the people Nebuchadnezzar had deported from Jerusalem to Babylon.

. . .

⁴ This is what the LORD of Armies, the God of Israel, says to all the exiles I deported from Jerusalem to Babylon: ⁵ "Build houses and live in them. Plant gardens and eat their produce. ⁶ Find wives for yourselves, and have sons and daughters. Find wives for your sons and give your daughters to men in marriage so that they may bear sons and daughters. Multiply there; do not decrease. ⁷ Pursue the well-being of the city I have deported you to. Pray to the LORD on its behalf, for when it thrives, you will thrive."

⁸ For this is what the LORD of Armies, the God of Israel, says: "Don't let your prophets who are among you and your diviners deceive you, and don't listen to the dreams you elicit from them, ⁹ for they are prophesying falsely to you in my name. I have not sent them." This is the LORD's declaration.

¹⁰ For this is what the LORD says: "When seventy years for Babylon are complete, I will attend to you and will confirm my promise concerning you to restore you to this place. ¹¹ For I know the plans I have for you"—this is the LORD's declaration—"plans for your well-being, not for disaster, to give you a future and a hope. ¹² You will call to me

and come and pray to me, and I will listen to you. [13] You will seek me and find me when you search for me with all your heart. [14] I will be found by you"—this is the Lord's declaration—"and I will restore your fortunes and gather you from all the nations and places where I banished you"—this is the Lord's declaration. "I will restore you to the place from which I deported you."

[15] You have said, "The Lord has raised up prophets for us in Babylon!" [16] But this is what the Lord says concerning the king sitting on David's throne and concerning all the people living in this city—that is, concerning your brothers who did not go with you into exile. [17] This is what the Lord of Armies says: "I am about to send sword, famine, and plague against them, and I will make them like rotten figs that are inedible because they are so bad. [18] I will pursue them with sword, famine, and plague. I will make them a horror to all the kingdoms of the earth—a curse and a desolation, an object of scorn and a disgrace among all the nations where I have banished them. [19] I will do this because they have not listened to my words"—this is the Lord's declaration—"the words that I sent to them with my servants the prophets time and time again. And you too have not listened." This is the Lord's declaration.

JEREMIAH 39:1, 9–18

[1] In the ninth year of King Zedekiah of Judah, in the tenth month, King Nebuchadnezzar of Babylon advanced against Jerusalem with his entire army and laid siege to it.

...

[9] Nebuzaradan, the captain of the guards, deported the rest of the people to Babylon—those who had remained in the city and those deserters who had defected to him along with the rest of the people who remained. [10] However, Nebuzaradan, the captain of the guards, left in the land of Judah some of the poor people who owned nothing, and he gave them vineyards and fields at that time.

JEREMIAH FREED BY NEBUCHADNEZZAR

[11] Speaking through Nebuzaradan, captain of the guards, King Nebuchadnezzar of Babylon gave orders concerning Jeremiah: [12] "Take him and look after him. Don't do him any harm, but do for him whatever he says." [13] Nebuzaradan, captain of the guards, Nebushazban the chief of staff, Nergal-sharezer the chief soothsayer, and all the captains of

Babylon's king [14] had Jeremiah brought from the guard's courtyard and turned him over to Gedaliah son of Ahikam, son of Shaphan, to take him home. So he settled among his own people.

[15] Now the word of the LORD had come to Jeremiah when he was confined in the guard's courtyard: [16] "Go tell Ebed-melech the Cushite, 'This is what the LORD of Armies, the God of Israel, says: I am about to fulfill my words for disaster and not for good against this city. They will take place before your eyes on that day. [17] But I will rescue you on that day—this is the LORD's declaration—and you will not be handed over to the men you dread. [18] Indeed, I will certainly deliver you so that you do not fall by the sword. Because you have trusted in me, you will retain your life like the spoils of war. This is the LORD's declaration.'"

RESPOND

01 WHERE DO I SEE GOD AT WORK IN
   JEREMIAH'S STORY?

_____
_____
_____
_____
_____
_____
_____
_____
_____

02 HOW DO I CONNECT TO JEREMIAH'S
   EXPERIENCES? IN WHAT WAYS DO HIS
   EXPERIENCES FEEL FOREIGN TO ME?

_____
_____
_____
_____
_____
_____
_____
_____
_____
_____

03 AFTER READING JEREMIAH'S STORY, WHAT DO I WANT TO CONTINUE TO MEDITATE ON?

_____
_____
_____
_____
_____
_____
_____
_____
_____
_____

GRACE DAY

TAKE THIS DAY TO CATCH UP ON
YOUR READING, PRAY, AND REST IN
THE PRESENCE OF THE LORD.

LONG AGO GOD SPOKE TO OUR
ANCESTORS BY THE PROPHETS AT
DIFFERENT TIMES AND IN DIFFERENT
WAYS. IN THESE LAST DAYS, HE HAS
SPOKEN TO US BY HIS SON. GOD HAS
APPOINTED HIM HEIR OF ALL THINGS
AND MADE THE UNIVERSE THROUGH HIM.

HEBREWS 1:1–2

WEEKLY

SCRIPTURE IS GOD BREATHED AND TRUE.
WHEN WE MEMORIZE IT, WE CARRY THE GOOD
NEWS OF JESUS WITH US WHEREVER WE GO.

FOR THIS PLAN, WE ARE MEMORIZING OUR KEY
PASSAGE, PSALM 8:3–4. WE WILL CONTINUE
WITH THE FINAL LINE.

SEE TIPS FOR MEMORIZING SCRIPTURE ON PAGE 236.

TRUTH

PSALM 8:3–4

WHEN I OBSERVE YOUR HEAVENS,
THE WORK OF YOUR FINGERS,
THE MOON AND THE STARS,
WHICH YOU SET IN PLACE,
WHAT IS A HUMAN BEING THAT YOU REMEMBER HIM,
A SON OF MAN THAT YOU LOOK AFTER HIM?

DANIEL

A MAN WHO REMAINED

FAITHFUL IN A FOREIGN LAND

DANIEL'S CAPTIVITY IN BABYLON

¹ In the third year of the reign of King Jehoiakim of Judah, King Nebuchadnezzar of Babylon came to Jerusalem and laid siege to it. ² The Lord handed King Jehoiakim of Judah over to him, along with some of the vessels from the house of God. Nebuchadnezzar carried them to the land of Babylon, to the house of his god, and put the vessels in the treasury of his god.

³ The king ordered Ashpenaz, his chief eunuch, to bring some of the Israelites from the royal family and from the nobility— ⁴ young men without any physical defect, good-looking, suitable for instruction in all wisdom, knowledgeable, perceptive, and capable of serving in the king's palace. He was to teach them the Chaldean language and literature. ⁵ The king assigned them daily provisions from the royal food and from the wine that he drank. They were to be trained for three years, and at the end of that time they were to attend the king. ⁶ Among them, from the Judahites, were Daniel, Hananiah, Mishael, and Azariah. ⁷ The chief eunuch gave them names; he gave the name Belteshazzar to Daniel, Shadrach to Hananiah, Meshach to Mishael, and Abednego to Azariah.

FAITHFULNESS IN BABYLON

⁸ Daniel determined that he would not defile himself with the king's food or with the wine he drank. So he asked permission from the chief eunuch not to defile himself. ⁹ God had granted Daniel kindness and compassion from the chief eunuch, ¹⁰ yet he said to Daniel, "I fear my lord the king, who assigned your food and drink. What if he sees your faces looking thinner than the other young men your age? You would endanger my life with the king."

¹¹ So Daniel said to the guard whom the chief eunuch had assigned to Daniel, Hananiah, Mishael, and Azariah, ¹² "Please test your servants for ten days. Let us be given vegetables to eat and water to drink. ¹³ Then examine our appearance and the appearance of the young men who are eating the king's food, and deal with your servants based on what you see." ¹⁴ He agreed with them about this and tested them for ten days. ¹⁵ At the end of ten days they looked better and healthier than all the young men who were eating the king's food. ¹⁶ So the guard continued to remove their food and the wine they were to drink and gave them vegetables.

FAITHFULNESS REWARDED

[17] God gave these four young men knowledge and understanding in every kind of literature and wisdom. Daniel also understood visions and dreams of every kind. [18] At the end of the time that the king had said to present them, the chief eunuch presented them to Nebuchadnezzar. [19] The king interviewed them, and among all of them, no one was found equal to Daniel, Hananiah, Mishael, and Azariah. So they began to attend the king. [20] In every matter of wisdom and understanding that the king consulted them about, he found them ten times better than all the magicians and mediums in his entire kingdom. [21] Daniel remained there until the first year of King Cyrus.

DANIEL 2:1-3, 10-19, 48

NEBUCHADNEZZAR'S DREAM

[1] In the second year of his reign, Nebuchadnezzar had dreams that troubled him, and sleep deserted him. [2] So the king gave orders to summon the magicians, mediums, sorcerers, and Chaldeans to tell the king his dreams. When they came and stood before the king, [3] he said to them, "I have had a dream and am anxious to understand it."

...

[10] The Chaldeans answered the king, "No one on earth can make known what the king requests. Consequently, no king, however great and powerful, has ever asked anything like this of any magician, medium, or Chaldean. [11] What the king is asking is so difficult that no one can make it known to him except the gods, whose dwelling is not with mortals." [12] Because of this, the king became violently angry and gave orders to destroy all the wise men of Babylon. [13] The decree was issued that the wise men were to be executed, and they searched for Daniel and his friends, to execute them.

[14] Then Daniel responded with tact and discretion to Arioch, the captain of the king's guard, who had gone out to execute the wise men of Babylon. [15] He asked Arioch, the king's officer, "Why is the decree from the king so harsh?" Then Arioch explained the situation to Daniel. [16] So Daniel went and asked the king to give him some time, so that he could give the king the interpretation.

[17] Then Daniel went to his house and told his friends Hananiah, Mishael, and Azariah about the matter, [18] urging them to ask the God of the

heavens for mercy concerning this mystery, so Daniel and his friends would not be destroyed with the rest of Babylon's wise men. [19] The mystery was then revealed to Daniel in a vision at night, and

DANIEL PRAISED THE GOD OF THE HEAVENS.

...

[48] Then the king promoted Daniel and gave him many generous gifts. He made him ruler over the entire province of Babylon and chief governor over all the wise men of Babylon.

DANIEL 6:1–22

THE PLOT AGAINST DANIEL

[1] Darius decided to appoint 120 satraps over the kingdom, stationed throughout the realm, [2] and over them three administrators, including Daniel. These satraps would be accountable to them so that the king would not be defrauded. [3] Daniel distinguished himself above the administrators and satraps because he had an extraordinary spirit, so the king planned to set him over the whole realm. [4] The administrators and satraps, therefore, kept trying to find a charge against Daniel regarding the kingdom. But they could find no charge or corruption, for he was trustworthy, and no negligence or corruption was found in him. [5] Then these men said, "We will never find any charge against this Daniel unless we find something against him concerning the law of his God."

[6] So the administrators and satraps went together to the king and said to him, "May King Darius live forever. [7] All the administrators of the kingdom—the prefects, satraps, advisers, and governors—have agreed that the king should establish an ordinance and enforce an edict that, for thirty days, anyone who petitions any god or man except you, the king, will be thrown into the lions' den. [8] Therefore, Your Majesty, establish the edict and sign the document so that, as a law of the Medes and Persians, it is irrevocable and cannot be changed." [9] So King Darius signed the written edict.

DANIEL IN THE LIONS' DEN

[10] When Daniel learned that the document had been signed, he went into his house. The windows in its upstairs room opened toward Jerusalem, and three times a day he got down on his knees, prayed, and gave thanks

to his God, just as he had done before. [11] Then these men went as a group and found Daniel petitioning and imploring his God. [12] So they approached the king and asked about his edict: "Didn't you sign an edict that for thirty days any person who petitions any god or man except you, the king, will be thrown into the lions' den?"

The king answered, "As a law of the Medes and Persians, the order stands and is irrevocable."

[13] Then they replied to the king, "Daniel, one of the Judean exiles, has ignored you, the king, and the edict you signed, for he prays three times a day." [14] As soon as the king heard this, he was very displeased; he set his mind on rescuing Daniel and made every effort until sundown to deliver him.

[15] Then these men went together to the king and said to him, "You know, Your Majesty, that it is a law of the Medes and Persians that no edict or ordinance the king establishes can be changed."

[16] So the king gave the order, and they brought Daniel and threw him into the lions' den. The king said to Daniel, "May your God, whom you continually serve, rescue you!" [17] A stone was brought and placed over the mouth of the den. The king sealed it with his own signet ring and with the signet rings of his nobles, so that nothing in regard to Daniel could be changed. [18] Then the king went to his palace and spent the night fasting. No diversions were brought to him, and he could not sleep.

DANIEL RELEASED

[19] At the first light of dawn the king got up and hurried to the lions' den. [20] When he reached the den, he cried out in anguish to Daniel. "Daniel, servant of the living God," the king said, "has your God, whom you continually serve, been able to rescue you from the lions?"

[21] Then Daniel spoke with the king: "May the king live forever. [22] My God sent his angel and shut the lions' mouths; and they haven't harmed me, for I was found innocent before him. And also before you, Your Majesty, I have not done harm."

RESPOND

1. WHERE DO I SEE GOD AT WORK IN DANIEL'S STORY?

2. HOW DO I CONNECT TO DANIEL'S EXPERIENCES? IN WHAT WAYS DO HIS EXPERIENCES FEEL FOREIGN TO ME?

3. AFTER READING DANIEL'S STORY, WHAT DO I WANT TO CONTINUE TO MEDITATE ON?

SHADRACH, MESHACH & ABEDNEGO

THREE MEN WHO REFUSED TO WORSHIP ANYONE BUT GOD

DANIEL 1:3-7, 17-20

³ The king ordered Ashpenaz, his chief eunuch, to bring some of the Israelites from the royal family and from the nobility— ⁴ young men without any physical defect, good-looking, suitable for instruction in all wisdom, knowledgeable, perceptive, and capable of serving in the king's palace. He was to teach them the Chaldean language and literature. ⁵ The king assigned them daily provisions from the royal food and from the wine that he drank. They were to be trained for three years, and at the end of that time they were to attend the king. ⁶ Among them, from the Judahites, were Daniel, Hananiah, Mishael, and Azariah. ⁷ The chief eunuch gave them names; he gave the name Belteshazzar to Daniel, Shadrach to Hananiah, Meshach to Mishael, and Abednego to Azariah.

...

FAITHFULNESS REWARDED

[17] God gave these four young men knowledge and understanding in every kind of literature and wisdom. Daniel also understood visions and dreams of every kind. [18] At the end of the time that the king had said to present them, the chief eunuch presented them to Nebuchadnezzar. [19] The king interviewed them, and among all of them, no one was found equal to Daniel, Hananiah, Mishael, and Azariah. So they began to attend the king. [20] In every matter of wisdom and understanding that the king consulted them about, he found them ten times better than all the magicians and mediums in his entire kingdom.

DANIEL 2:49

At Daniel's request, the king appointed Shadrach, Meshach, and Abednego to manage the province of Babylon. But Daniel remained at the king's court.

DANIEL 3

NEBUCHADNEZZAR'S GOLD STATUE

[1] King Nebuchadnezzar made a gold statue, ninety feet high and nine feet wide. He set it up on the plain of Dura in the province of Babylon. [2] King Nebuchadnezzar sent word to assemble the satraps, prefects, governors, advisers, treasurers, judges, magistrates, and all the rulers of the provinces to attend the dedication of the statue King Nebuchadnezzar had set up. [3] So the satraps, prefects, governors, advisers, treasurers, judges, magistrates, and all the rulers of the provinces assembled for the dedication of the statue the king had set up. Then they stood before the statue Nebuchadnezzar had set up.

[4] A herald loudly proclaimed, "People of every nation and language, you are commanded: [5] When you hear the sound of the horn, flute, zither, lyre, harp, drum, and every kind of music, you are to fall facedown and worship the gold statue that King Nebuchadnezzar has set up. [6] But whoever does not fall down and worship will immediately be thrown into a furnace of blazing fire."

[7] Therefore, when all the people heard the sound of the horn, flute, zither, lyre, harp, and every kind of music, people of every nation and language fell down and worshiped the gold statue that King Nebuchadnezzar had set up.

⁸ Some Chaldeans took this occasion to come forward and maliciously accuse the Jews. ⁹ They said to King Nebuchadnezzar, "May the king live forever. ¹⁰ You as king have issued a decree that everyone who hears the sound of the horn, flute, zither, lyre, harp, drum, and every kind of music must fall down and worship the gold statue. ¹¹ Whoever does not fall down and worship will be thrown into a furnace of blazing fire. ¹² There are some Jews you have appointed to manage the province of Babylon: Shadrach, Meshach, and Abednego. These men have ignored you, the king;

THEY DO NOT SERVE YOUR GODS OR WORSHIP THE GOLD STATUE YOU HAVE SET UP."

¹³ Then in a furious rage Nebuchadnezzar gave orders to bring in Shadrach, Meshach, and Abednego. So these men were brought before the king. ¹⁴ Nebuchadnezzar asked them, "Shadrach, Meshach, and Abednego, is it true that you don't serve my gods or worship the gold statue I have set up? ¹⁵ Now if you're ready, when you hear the sound of the horn, flute, zither, lyre, harp, drum, and every kind of music, fall down and worship the statue I made. But if you don't worship it, you will immediately be thrown into a furnace of blazing fire—and who is the god who can rescue you from my power?"

¹⁶ Shadrach, Meshach, and Abednego replied to the king, "Nebuchadnezzar, we don't need to give you an answer to this question. ¹⁷ If the God we serve exists, then he can rescue us from the furnace of blazing fire, and he can rescue us from the power of you, the king. ¹⁸ But even if he does not rescue us, we want you as king to know that we will not serve your gods or worship the gold statue you set up."

¹⁹ Then Nebuchadnezzar was filled with rage, and the expression on his face changed toward Shadrach, Meshach, and Abednego. He gave orders to heat the furnace seven times more than was customary, ²⁰ and he commanded some of the best soldiers in his army to tie up Shadrach, Meshach, and Abednego and throw them into the furnace of blazing fire. ²¹ So these men, in their trousers, robes, head coverings, and other clothes, were tied up and thrown into the furnace of blazing fire. ²² Since the king's command was so urgent and the furnace extremely hot, the raging flames killed those men who carried up Shadrach, Meshach, and

Abednego. [23] And these three men, Shadrach, Meshach, and Abednego fell, bound, into the furnace of blazing fire.

DELIVERED FROM THE FIRE

[24] Then King Nebuchadnezzar jumped up in alarm. He said to his advisers, "Didn't we throw three men, bound, into the fire?"

"Yes, of course, Your Majesty," they replied to the king.

[25] He exclaimed, "Look! I see four men, not tied, walking around in the fire unharmed; and the fourth looks like a son of the gods."

[26] Nebuchadnezzar then approached the door of the furnace of blazing fire and called, "Shadrach, Meshach, and Abednego, you servants of the Most High God—come out!" So Shadrach, Meshach, and Abednego came out of the fire. [27] When the satraps, prefects, governors, and the king's advisers gathered around, they saw that the fire had no effect on the bodies of these men: not a hair of their heads was singed, their robes were unaffected, and there was no smell of fire on them. [28] Nebuchadnezzar exclaimed, "Praise to the God of Shadrach, Meshach, and Abednego! He sent his angel and rescued his servants who trusted in him. They violated the king's command and risked their lives rather than serve or worship any god except their own God. [29] Therefore I issue a decree that anyone of any people, nation, or language who says anything offensive against the God of Shadrach, Meshach, and Abednego will be torn limb from limb and his house made a garbage dump. For there is no other god who is able to deliver like this." [30] Then the king rewarded Shadrach, Meshach, and Abednego in the province of Babylon.

RESPOND

DATE   /   /

1. WHERE DO I SEE GOD AT WORK IN SHADRACH, MESHACH, AND ABEDNEGO'S STORY?

2. HOW DO I CONNECT TO SHADRACH, MESHACH, AND ABEDNEGO'S EXPERIENCES? IN WHAT WAYS DO THEIR EXPERIENCES FEEL FOREIGN TO ME?

3. AFTER READING SHADRACH, MESHACH, AND ABEDNEGO'S STORY, WHAT DO I WANT TO CONTINUE TO MEDITATE ON?

HE READS TRUTH   DAY 44   213

ZERUBBABEL

DAY 45  WEEK 7

EZRA 3:1-8

SACRIFICE RESTORED

¹ When the seventh month arrived, and the Israelites were in their towns, the people gathered as one in Jerusalem. ² Jeshua son of Jozadak and his brothers the priests along with Zerubbabel son of Shealtiel and his brothers began to build the altar of Israel's God in order to offer burnt offerings on it, as it is written in the law of Moses, the man of God. ³ They set up the altar on its foundation and offered burnt offerings for the morning and evening on it to the LORD even though they feared the surrounding peoples. ⁴ They celebrated the Festival of Shelters as prescribed, and offered burnt offerings each day, based on the number specified by ordinance for each festival day. ⁵ After that, they offered the regular burnt offering and the offerings for the beginning of each month and for all the LORD's appointed holy occasions, as well as the freewill offerings brought to the LORD.

⁶ On the first day of the seventh month they began to offer burnt offerings to the LORD, even though the foundation of the LORD's temple had not yet been laid. ⁷ They gave money to the stonecutters and artisans, and gave food, drink, and oil to the people of Sidon and Tyre, so they would bring cedar wood from Lebanon to Joppa by sea, according to the authorization given them by King Cyrus of Persia.

REBUILDING THE TEMPLE

⁸ In the second month of the second year after they arrived at God's house in Jerusalem, Zerubbabel son of Shealtiel, Jeshua son of Jozadak, and the rest of their brothers, including the priests, the Levites, and all who had returned to Jerusalem from the captivity, began to build. They appointed the Levites who were twenty years old or more to supervise the work on the LORD's house.

EZRA 5:2

Zerubbabel son of Shealtiel and Jeshua son of Jozadak began to rebuild God's house in Jerusalem. The prophets of God were with them, helping them.

HAGGAI 1:1-4, 7-8, 12-15

COMMAND TO REBUILD THE TEMPLE

¹ In the second year of King Darius, on the first day of the sixth month, the word of the LORD came through the prophet Haggai to

Zerubbabel son of Shealtiel, the governor of Judah, and to Joshua son of Jehozadak, the high priest:

² "The LORD of Armies says this: These people say: The time has not come for the house of the LORD to be rebuilt."

³ The word of the LORD came through the prophet Haggai: ⁴ "Is it a time for you yourselves to live in your paneled houses, while this house lies in ruins?"

. . .

⁷ The LORD of Armies says this: "Think carefully about your ways. ⁸ Go up into the hills, bring down lumber, and build the house; and I will be pleased with it and be glorified," says the LORD.

. . .

THE PEOPLE'S RESPONSE

¹² Then Zerubbabel son of Shealtiel, the high priest Joshua son of Jehozadak, and the entire remnant of the people obeyed the LORD their God and the words of the prophet Haggai, because the LORD their God had sent him. So the people feared the LORD.

¹³ Then Haggai, the LORD's messenger, delivered the LORD's message to the people: "I am with you—this is the LORD's declaration."

¹⁴ The LORD roused the spirit of Zerubbabel son of Shealtiel, governor of Judah, the spirit of the high priest Joshua son of Jehozadak, and the spirit of all the remnant of the people. They began work on the house of the LORD of Armies, their God, ¹⁵ on the twenty-fourth day of the sixth month, in the second year of King Darius.

HAGGAI 2:1-5, 20-23

ENCOURAGEMENT AND PROMISE

¹ On the twenty-first day of the seventh month, the word of the LORD came through the prophet Haggai: ² "Speak to Zerubbabel son of Shealtiel, governor of Judah, to the high priest Joshua son of Jehozadak, and to the remnant of the people: ³ 'Who is left among you who saw this house in its former glory? How does it look to you now? Doesn't it seem to you like nothing by comparison? ⁴ Even so, be strong, Zerubbabel—this

is the Lord's declaration. Be strong, Joshua son of Jehozadak, high priest. Be strong, all you people of the land—this is the Lord's declaration.

WORK! FOR I AM WITH YOU—THE DECLARATION OF THE LORD OF ARMIES.

[5] This is the promise I made to you when you came out of Egypt, and my Spirit is present among you; don't be afraid.'"

...

PROMISE TO ZERUBBABEL

[20] The word of the Lord came to Haggai a second time on the twenty-fourth day of the month: [21] "Speak to Zerubbabel, governor of Judah: I am going to shake the heavens and the earth. [22] I will overturn royal thrones and destroy the power of the Gentile kingdoms. I will overturn chariots and their riders. Horses and their riders will fall, each by his brother's sword. [23] On that day"—this is the declaration of the Lord of Armies—"I will take you, Zerubbabel son of Shealtiel, my servant"—this is the Lord's declaration—"and make you like my signet ring, for I have chosen you." This is the declaration of the Lord of Armies.

ZECHARIAH 4:8–10

[8] Then the word of the Lord came to me: [9] "Zerubbabel's hands have laid the foundation of this house, and his hands will complete it. Then you will know that the Lord of Armies has sent me to you. [10] For who despises the day of small things? These seven eyes of the Lord, which scan throughout the whole earth, will rejoice when they see the ceremonial stone in Zerubbabel's hand."

RESPOND

1. WHERE DO I SEE GOD AT WORK IN ZERUBBABEL'S STORY?

2. HOW DO I CONNECT TO ZERUBBABEL'S EXPERIENCES? IN WHAT WAYS DO HIS EXPERIENCES FEEL FOREIGN TO ME?

3. AFTER READING ZERUBBABEL'S STORY, WHAT DO I WANT TO CONTINUE TO MEDITATE ON?

ESTHER

THE FAVORED QUEEN WHO SAVED HER PEOPLE

ESTHER GAINED FAVOR IN THE EYES OF EVERYONE

WHO SAW HER. —ESTHER 2:15

THE SEARCH FOR A NEW QUEEN

¹ Some time later, when King Ahasuerus's rage had cooled down, he remembered Vashti, what she had done, and what was decided against her. ² The king's personal attendants suggested, "Let a search be made for beautiful young virgins for the king. ³ Let the king appoint commissioners in each province of his kingdom, so that they may gather all the beautiful young virgins to the harem at the fortress of Susa. Put them under the supervision of Hegai, the king's eunuch, keeper of the women, and give them the required beauty treatments. ⁴ Then the young woman who pleases the king will become queen instead of Vashti." This suggestion pleased the king, and he did accordingly.

⁵ In the fortress of Susa, there was a Jewish man named Mordecai son of Jair, son of Shimei, son of Kish, a Benjaminite. ⁶ Kish had been taken into exile from Jerusalem with the other captives when King Nebuchadnezzar of Babylon took King Jeconiah of Judah into exile. ⁷ Mordecai was the legal guardian of his cousin Hadassah (that is, Esther), because she had no father or mother. The young woman had a beautiful figure and was extremely good-looking. When her father and mother died, Mordecai had adopted her as his own daughter.

⁸ When the king's command and edict became public knowledge and when many young women were gathered at the fortress of Susa under Hegai's supervision, Esther was taken to the palace, into the supervision of Hegai, keeper of the women. ⁹ The young woman pleased him and gained his favor so that he accelerated the process of the beauty treatments and the special diet that she received. He assigned seven hand-picked female servants to her from the palace and transferred her and her servants to the harem's best quarters.

¹⁰ Esther did not reveal her ethnicity or her family background, because Mordecai had ordered her not to make them known. ¹¹ Every day Mordecai took a walk in front of the harem's courtyard to learn how Esther was doing and to see what was happening to her.

. . .

ESTHER BECOMES QUEEN

¹⁵ Esther was the daughter of Abihail, the uncle of Mordecai who had adopted her as his own daughter. When her turn came to go to the king,

she did not ask for anything except what Hegai, the king's eunuch, keeper of the women, suggested. Esther gained favor in the eyes of everyone who saw her.

[16] She was taken to King Ahasuerus in the palace in the tenth month, the month Tebeth, in the seventh year of his reign. [17] The king loved Esther more than all the other women. She won more favor and approval from him than did any of the other virgins. He placed the royal crown on her head and made her queen in place of Vashti. [18] The king held a great banquet for all his officials and staff. It was Esther's banquet. He freed his provinces from tax payments and gave gifts worthy of the king's bounty.

ESTHER 3:1-6

HAMAN'S PLAN TO KILL THE JEWS

[1] After all this took place, King Ahasuerus honored Haman, son of Hammedatha the Agagite. He promoted him in rank and gave him a higher position than all the other officials. [2] The entire royal staff at the King's Gate bowed down and paid homage to Haman, because the king had commanded this to be done for him. But Mordecai would not bow down or pay homage. [3] The members of the royal staff at the King's Gate asked Mordecai, "Why are you disobeying the king's command?" [4] When they had warned him day after day and he still would not listen to them, they told Haman in order to see if Mordecai's actions would be tolerated, since he had told them he was a Jew.

[5] When Haman saw that Mordecai was not bowing down or paying him homage, he was filled with rage. [6] And when he learned of Mordecai's ethnic identity, it seemed repugnant to Haman to do away with Mordecai alone. He planned to destroy all of Mordecai's people, the Jews, throughout Ahasuerus's kingdom.

ESTHER 4:4-17

[4] Esther's female servants and her eunuchs came and reported the news to her, and the queen was overcome with fear. She sent clothes for Mordecai to wear so that he would take off his sackcloth, but he did not accept them. [5] Esther summoned Hathach, one of the king's eunuchs who attended her, and dispatched him to Mordecai to learn what he was doing and why. [6] So Hathach went out to Mordecai in the city square in front of the King's Gate. [7] Mordecai told him everything that had

happened as well as the exact amount of money Haman had promised to pay the royal treasury for the slaughter of the Jews.

NOTES

[8] Mordecai also gave him a copy of the written decree issued in Susa ordering their destruction, so that Hathach might show it to Esther, explain it to her, and command her to approach the king, implore his favor, and plead with him personally for her people. [9] Hathach came and repeated Mordecai's response to Esther.

[10] Esther spoke to Hathach and commanded him to tell Mordecai, [11] "All the royal officials and the people of the royal provinces know that one law applies to every man or woman who approaches the king in the inner courtyard and who has not been summoned—the death penalty—unless the king extends the gold scepter, allowing that person to live. I have not been summoned to appear before the king for the last thirty days."
[12] Esther's response was reported to Mordecai.

[13] Mordecai told the messenger to reply to Esther, "Don't think that you will escape the fate of all the Jews because you are in the king's palace.
[14] If you keep silent at this time, relief and deliverance will come to the Jewish people from another place, but you and your father's family will be destroyed. Who knows,

PERHAPS YOU HAVE COME TO YOUR ROYAL POSITION FOR SUCH A TIME AS THIS."

[15] Esther sent this reply to Mordecai: [16] "Go and assemble all the Jews who can be found in Susa and fast for me. Don't eat or drink for three days, night or day. I and my female servants will also fast in the same way. After that, I will go to the king even if it is against the law. If I perish, I perish."
[17] So Mordecai went and did everything Esther had commanded him.

ESTHER 8:3–8

[3] Then Esther addressed the king again. She fell at his feet, wept, and begged him to revoke the evil of Haman the Agagite and his plot he had devised against the Jews. [4] The king extended the gold scepter toward Esther, so she got up and stood before the king.

[5] She said, "If it pleases the king and I have found favor with him, if the matter seems right to the king and I am pleasing in his eyes, let a

royal edict be written. Let it revoke the documents the scheming Haman son of Hammedatha the Agagite wrote to destroy the Jews who are in all the king's provinces. [6] For how could I bear to see the disaster that would come on my people? How could I bear to see the destruction of my relatives?"

[7] King Ahasuerus said to Esther the queen and to Mordecai the Jew, "Look, I have given Haman's estate to Esther, and he was hanged on the gallows because he attacked the Jews. [8] Write in the king's name whatever pleases you concerning the Jews, and seal it with the royal signet ring. A document written in the king's name and sealed with the royal signet ring cannot be revoked."

RESPOND

DATE   /   /

1. WHERE DO I SEE GOD AT WORK IN ESTHER'S STORY?

2. HOW DO I CONNECT TO ESTHER'S EXPERIENCES? IN WHAT WAYS DO HER EXPERIENCES FEEL FOREIGN TO ME?

3. AFTER READING ESTHER'S STORY, WHAT DO I WANT TO CONTINUE TO MEDITATE ON?

NEHEMIAH

THE GOVERNOR WHO REBUILT JERUSALEM'S WALLS

EZRA 2:1–2

THE EXILES WHO RETURNED

[1] These now are the people of the province who came from those captive exiles King Nebuchadnezzar of Babylon had deported to Babylon. They returned to Jerusalem and Judah, each to his own town. [2] They came with Zerubbabel, Jeshua, Nehemiah, Seraiah, Reelaiah, Mordecai, Bilshan, Mispar, Bigvai, Rehum, and Baanah.

NEHEMIAH 1

[1] The words of Nehemiah son of Hacaliah:

NEWS FROM JERUSALEM

During the month of Chislev in the twentieth year, when I was in the fortress city of Susa, [2] Hanani, one of my brothers, arrived with men from Judah, and I questioned them about Jerusalem and the Jewish remnant that had survived the exile. [3] They said to me, "The remnant in the province, who survived the exile, are in great trouble and disgrace. Jerusalem's wall has been broken down, and its gates have been burned."

NEHEMIAH'S PRAYER

[4] When I heard these words, I sat down and wept. I mourned for a number of days, fasting and praying before the God of the heavens. [5] I said,

LORD, the God of the heavens, the great and awe-inspiring God who keeps his gracious covenant with those who love him and keep his commands, [6] let your eyes be open and your ears be attentive to hear your servant's prayer that I now pray to you day and night for your servants, the Israelites. I confess the sins we have committed against you. Both I and my father's family have sinned. [7] We have acted corruptly toward you and have not kept the commands, statutes, and ordinances you gave your servant Moses. [8] Please remember what you commanded your servant Moses: "If you are unfaithful, I will scatter you among the peoples. [9] But if you return to me and carefully observe my commands, even though your exiles were banished to the farthest horizon, I will gather them from there and bring them to the place where I chose to have my name dwell." [10] They are your servants and your people. You redeemed them by your great power and strong hand. [11] Please, Lord, let your ear be attentive to the prayer of your servant and to that of your servants who delight to revere your name. Give your servant success today, and grant him compassion in the presence of this man.

At the time, I was the king's cupbearer.

NEHEMIAH 2:1-6

NEHEMIAH SENT TO JERUSALEM

[1] During the month of Nisan in the twentieth year of King Artaxerxes, when wine was set before him, I took the wine and gave it to the king. I had never been sad in his presence, [2] so the king said to me, "Why do you look so sad, when you aren't sick? This is nothing but sadness of heart."

I was overwhelmed with fear [3] and replied to the king, "May the king live forever! Why should I not be sad when the city where my ancestors are buried lies in ruins and its gates have been destroyed by fire?"

[4] Then the king asked me, "What is your request?"

So I prayed to the God of the heavens [5] and answered the king, "If it pleases the king, and if your servant has found favor with you,

SEND ME TO JUDAH AND TO THE CITY WHERE MY ANCESTORS ARE BURIED, SO THAT I MAY REBUILD IT."

[6] The king, with the queen seated beside him, asked me, "How long will your journey take, and when will you return?" So I gave him a definite time, and it pleased the king to send me.

NEHEMIAH 6:1-4

ATTEMPTS TO DISCOURAGE THE BUILDERS

[1] When Sanballat, Tobiah, Geshem the Arab, and the rest of our enemies heard that I had rebuilt the wall and that no gap was left in it—though at that time I had not installed the doors in the city gates— [2] Sanballat and Geshem sent me a message: "Come, let's meet together in the villages of the Ono Valley." They were planning to harm me.

[3] So I sent messengers to them, saying, "I am doing important work and cannot come down. Why should the work cease while I leave it and go down to you?" [4] Four times they sent me the same proposal, and I gave them the same reply.

NEHEMIAH 13:1-14

NEHEMIAH'S FURTHER REFORMS

[1] At that time the book of Moses was read publicly to the people. The command was found written in it that no Ammonite or Moabite should ever enter the assembly of God, [2] because they did not meet the Israelites with food and water. Instead, they hired Balaam against them to curse them, but our God turned the curse into a blessing. [3] When they heard the law, they separated all those of mixed descent from Israel.

[4] Now before this, the priest Eliashib had been put in charge of the storerooms of the house of our God. He was a relative of Tobiah [5] and had prepared a large room for him where they had previously stored the grain

offerings, the frankincense, the articles, and the tenths of grain, new wine, and fresh oil prescribed for the Levites, singers, and gatekeepers, along with the contributions for the priests.

⁶ While all this was happening, I was not in Jerusalem, because I had returned to King Artaxerxes of Babylon in the thirty-second year of his reign. It was only later that I asked the king for a leave of absence ⁷ so I could return to Jerusalem. Then I discovered the evil that Eliashib had done on behalf of Tobiah by providing him a room in the courts of God's house. ⁸ I was greatly displeased and threw all of Tobiah's household possessions out of the room. ⁹ I ordered that the rooms be purified, and I had the articles of the house of God restored there, along with the grain offering and frankincense. ¹⁰ I also found out that because the portions for the Levites had not been given, each of the Levites and the singers performing the service had gone back to his own field. ¹¹ Therefore, I rebuked the officials, asking, "Why has the house of God been neglected?" I gathered the Levites and singers together and stationed them at their posts. ¹² Then all Judah brought a tenth of the grain, new wine, and fresh oil into the storehouses. ¹³ I appointed as treasurers over the storehouses the priest Shelemiah, the scribe Zadok, and Pedaiah of the Levites, with Hanan son of Zaccur, son of Mattaniah to assist them, because they were considered trustworthy. They were responsible for the distribution to their colleagues.

¹⁴ Remember me for this, my God, and don't erase the deeds of faithful love I have done for the house of my God and for its services.

RESPOND

DATE   /   /

1. WHERE DO I SEE GOD AT WORK IN NEHEMIAH'S STORY?

2. HOW DO I CONNECT TO NEHEMIAH'S EXPERIENCES? IN WHAT WAYS DO HIS EXPERIENCES FEEL FOREIGN TO ME?

3. AFTER READING NEHEMIAH'S STORY, WHAT DO I WANT TO CONTINUE TO MEDITATE ON?

GRACE DAY

TAKE THIS DAY TO CATCH UP ON
YOUR READING, PRAY, AND REST IN
THE PRESENCE OF THE LORD.

THEREFORE, BROTHERS AND SISTERS,
BE PATIENT UNTIL THE LORD'S COMING.
SEE HOW THE FARMER WAITS FOR THE
PRECIOUS FRUIT OF THE EARTH AND
IS PATIENT WITH IT UNTIL IT RECEIVES
THE EARLY AND THE LATE RAINS. YOU
ALSO MUST BE PATIENT. STRENGTHEN
YOUR HEARTS, BECAUSE THE LORD'S
COMING IS NEAR.

JAMES 5:7–8

WEEKLY

SCRIPTURE IS GOD BREATHED AND TRUE.
WHEN WE MEMORIZE IT, WE CARRY THE GOOD
NEWS OF JESUS WITH US WHEREVER WE GO.

FOR THIS PLAN, WE HAVE BEEN MEMORIZING
OUR KEY PASSAGE, PSALM 8:3–4. TO CLOSE,
SPEND TIME COMMITTING THE ENTIRE
PASSAGE TO MEMORY.

SEE TIPS FOR MEMORIZING SCRIPTURE ON PAGE 236.

TRUTH

PSALM 8:3-4

WHEN I OBSERVE YOUR HEAVENS,
THE WORK OF YOUR FINGERS,
THE MOON AND THE STARS,
WHICH YOU SET IN PLACE,
WHAT IS A HUMAN BEING THAT YOU REMEMBER HIM,
A SON OF MAN THAT YOU LOOK AFTER HIM?

BENEDICTION

DO NOT PASS AWAY FROM THIS EARTH WITH
ALL THOSE PLEASANT MEMORIES OF GOD'S
LOVINGKINDNESS  TO BE BURIED WITH
YOU IN YOUR COFFIN; BUT LET
YOUR CHILDREN, AND YOUR
CHILDREN'S CHILDREN, KNOW WHAT THE
EVERLASTING GOD DID FOR YOU.

CHARLES H. SPURGEON

Tips for Memorizing Scripture

At He Reads Truth, we believe Scripture memorization is an important discipline in your walk with God. Committing God's Truth to memory means we carry it with us and we can minister to others wherever we go. As you approach the Weekly Truth passage in this book, try these memorization tips to see which techniques work best for you.

STUDY IT

Study the passage in its biblical context, and ask yourself a few questions before you begin to memorize it: What does this passage say? What does it mean? How would I say this in my own words? What does it teach me about God? Understanding what the passage means helps you know why it is important to carry it with you wherever you go.

Break the passage into smaller sections, memorizing a phrase at a time.

PRAY IT

Use the passage you are memorizing as a prompt for prayer.

WRITE IT

Dedicate a notebook to Scripture memorization, and write the passage over and over again.

Diagram the passage after you write it out. Place a square around the verbs, underline the nouns, and circle any adjectives or adverbs. Say the passage aloud several times, emphasizing the verbs as you repeat it. Then do the same thing again with the nouns, then the adjectives and adverbs.

Write out the first letter of each word in the passage somewhere you can reference it throughout the week as you work on your memorization.

Use a whiteboard to write out the passage. Erase a few words at a time as you continue to repeat it aloud. Keep erasing parts of the passage until you have it all committed to memory.

CREATE

If you can, make up a tune for the passage to sing as you go about your day, or try singing it to the tune of a favorite song.

Use hand signals or signs to come up with associations for each word or phrase and repeat the movements as you practice.

SAY IT

Repeat the passage out loud to yourself as you are going through the rhythm of your day—getting ready, pouring your coffee, waiting in traffic, or making dinner.

Listen to the passage read aloud to you.

Record a voice memo on your phone, and listen to it throughout the day or play it on an audio Bible.

SHARE IT

Memorize the passage with a friend, family member, or mentor. Spontaneously challenge each other to recite the passage, or pick a time to review your passage and practice saying it from memory together.

Send the passage as an encouraging text to a friend, testing yourself as you type to see how much you have memorized so far.

KEEP AT IT

Set reminders on your phone to prompt you to practice your passage.

Keep a stack of note cards with Scripture you are memorizing by your bed. Practice reciting what you've memorized previously before you go to sleep, ending with the passages you are currently learning. If you wake up in the middle of the night, review them again instead of grabbing your phone. Read them out loud before you get out of bed in the morning.

CSB BOOK ABBREVIATIONS

OLD TESTAMENT

GN Genesis	**JB** Job	**HAB** Habakkuk	**PHP** Philippians
EX Exodus	**PS** Psalms	**ZPH** Zephaniah	**COL** Colossians
LV Leviticus	**PR** Proverbs	**HG** Haggai	**1TH** 1 Thessalonians
NM Numbers	**EC** Ecclesiastes	**ZCH** Zechariah	**2TH** 2 Thessalonians
DT Deuteronomy	**SG** Song of Solomon	**MAL** Malachi	**1TM** 1 Timothy
JOS Joshua	**IS** Isaiah		**2TM** 2 Timothy
JDG Judges	**JR** Jeremiah	### NEW TESTAMENT	**TI** Titus
RU Ruth	**LM** Lamentations	**MT** Matthew	**PHM** Philemon
1SM 1 Samuel	**EZK** Ezekiel	**MK** Mark	**HEB** Hebrews
2SM 2 Samuel	**DN** Daniel	**LK** Luke	**JMS** James
1KG 1 Kings	**HS** Hosea	**JN** John	**1PT** 1 Peter
2KG 2 Kings	**JL** Joel	**AC** Acts	**2PT** 2 Peter
1CH 1 Chronicles	**AM** Amos	**RM** Romans	**1JN** 1 John
2CH 2 Chronicles	**OB** Obadiah	**1CO** 1 Corinthians	**2JN** 2 John
EZR Ezra	**JNH** Jonah	**2CO** 2 Corinthians	**3JN** 3 John
NEH Nehemiah	**MC** Micah	**GL** Galatians	**JD** Jude
EST Esther	**NAH** Nahum	**EPH** Ephesians	**RV** Revelation

BIBLIOGRAPHY

Spurgeon, Charles H. "Remembering God's Works." Metropolitan Tabernacle Pulpit, October 4, 1877.

You just spent 49 days in the Word of God.

My favorite day of this reading plan:

How did I find delight in God's Word?

One thing I learned about God:

What was God doing in my life during this study?

What did I learn that I want to share with someone else?

A specific passage or verse that encouraged me:

A specific passage or verse that challenged and convicted me: